TESHUVAH

═ *TESHUVAH* ═

A GUIDE FOR THE
NEWLY OBSERVANT JEW

Adin Steinsaltz

THE FREE PRESS
A Division of Macmillan, Inc.
NEW YORK

Collier Macmillan Publishers
LONDON

The Free Press
A Division of Macmillan, Inc.
866 Third Avenue, New York, N.Y. 10022

Collier Macmillan Canada, Inc.

Printed in the United States of America

printing number

2   3   4   5   6   7   8   9   10

Library of Congress Cataloging-in-Publication Data

Steinsaltz, Adin.
  Teshuvah : a guide for the newly observant Jew.

  Translation of: Teshuvah.
  Bibliography: p.
  Includes index.
  1. Jewish way of life. 2. Jews—Return to Orthodox
Judaism. I. Swirsky, Michael. II. Title.
BM723.S713 1987   296.7′4   86-31994
ISBN 0-02-931150-0

Edited and translated by Michael Swirsky

Contents

Contents

Preface

This book is not intended as a call to *teshuvah*, nor is it an attempt to convince anyone to take that path. Rather, it is addressed to those who are already considering *teshuvah*, those who have already resolved to undertake it, or those who have already begun. The book is offered to the *ba'al teshuvah* as advice and guidance in dealing with some of the difficulties likely to be encountered along the way. (Use of the terms *ba'al teshuvah* and the pronoun *he* generically is not intended to exclude women from this experience.) Some of these difficulties are of a practical nature: how to behave in particular circumstances. Most are matters of principle and spiritual orientation: what the observances mean, how they are related, and, once embarked on the path of *teshuvah*, how one is to relate to self, family, and the surrounding society.

It is not my intention to encompass "the whole Torah" but only to deal with certain issues that seem essential. From a practical point of view, this book does not pretend to be a detailed halakhic work. It sets forth only the main outlines and underlying principles; when it goes into detail, it does so only in regard to certain particularly sensitive points. One who wishes to study these matters in greater depth would do well to turn to the many available halakhic reference works. Furthermore, there are many rabbis and people learned in Torah to whom anyone serious about *teshuvah* can turn for help. In some of the areas of observance dealt with here, there are also differences of opinion and custom, making further study and counsel particularly important.

I was urged to write this book for people in a variety of quarters. I can only hope it will serve its purpose.

The book is gratefully dedicated to Rabbis Nahum Shmaryahu Sassonkin, Shlomo Hayim Kesselman, and Dov Eliezrov, who many years ago lavished love, time, and patience on one particular boy.

PART I

1

The Meaning of *Teshuvah*

Teshuvah occupies a central place in Judaism and has many facets. As individuals differ from one another, so too do their modes of *teshuvah*, in both motive and form of expression. Broadly defined, *teshuvah* is more than just repentance from sin; it is a spiritual reawakening, a desire to strengthen the connection between oneself and the sacred. The effectiveness of *teshuvah* is thus frequently a function of one's sense of distance from the sacred. The greater the distance, the greater the potential movement toward renewed connectedness. As one Jewish sage put it, A rope that is cut and retied is doubly strong at the point where it was severed.

This movement of the soul toward renewed connectedness can also come about in one who has never sinned yet who feels called upon to draw closer to holiness. For at the root of the notion of *teshuvah* lies the concept of return (*shivah*)—return, not only to the past (one's own, or one's ancestors'), but to the Divine source of all being: "You shall return [*shavta*] to the Lord your God."

All forms of *teshuvah*, however diverse and complex, have a common core: the belief that human beings have it in their power to effect inward change. Many factors conspire to distance one from the Creator, education and habit among them; habit, in turn, has many causes. The rule that "transgression begets transgression" reflects not only an assumption about the transcendent foundations of human life, but also a sober view of reality. There is a causal connection: one cannot extricate oneself all at once from both the inward and outward consequences of one's actions. For this reason, one transgression creates a situation in which a second seems logical, natural, virtually inevitable. A way of life remote from religious observance not only makes such observance difficult, but also by its own inner logic makes it progressively more difficult. Yet, despite these behavioral laws, there remains *teshuvah:* the ever-present possibility of changing one's life and the very direction of one's life. According to the Talmudic sages, this possibility of altering reality after the fact, which is one of the mysteries of all being, was created before the world itself. Before the laws of nature came into existence—"before the mountains were born," as the Divine poet put it—a principle even more fundamental and more exalted was proclaimed: that change—*teshuvah*—is possible.

Many books and articles have been written about *teshuvah,* providing detailed analyses of the various stages of the process from start to finish. Yet, for all this elaboration, a few fundamental principles underlie all forms and levels of *teshuvah,* whether its starting point be exalted or lowly, whether it aims at a high level of spiritual perfection or at more modest objectives. In fact, two essentials are found in every kind of *teshuvah:* the renunciation of a regretted past and the adoption of a better path to be followed henceforth. Put concretely, *teshuvah* is simply a turning, be it a complete, abrupt change of direction or a series of smaller turns, not all of equal significance. Implicit in our petitions for *teshuvah* and forgiveness, repeated by all in our thrice-daily services, is the possibility of *some* kind of turning. As a rule, the more settled and tranquil a person's life, the less sharp a turn he is likely to make. Yet, often we surprise ourselves, and it is not unusual to realize only with the wisdom of hindsight what our true turning points have been.

There are, as we have said, two factors that make the turning possible: the realization that the past, whatever it may have been, is imperfect and in need of correction; and the decision to change direction, to go a different way in the future. The nature, exact description, and possible consequences of this turning are discussed in the literature of *teshuvah*.

The recognition of the need to turn comes about in different ways. Sometimes one is overcome by a sense of sinfulness, of blemish, of defilement, which results in a powerful desire for escape and purification. But the desire to turn can also take more subtle forms, feelings of imperfection or unrealized potential, which spur a search for something better. As a rule, the greater the initial feeling of past inadequacy, the sharper the turn is likely to be, sometimes to the point of extremism and total inversion. When the sense of discomfort or incompleteness is more subdued, the resulting turn will generally be more moderate, both in its speed and its sharpness. But, whatever the primary feeling regarding the past, the desire to do *teshuvah* always springs from some sense of unease or disquiet. The great obstacle in the way of *teshuvah*, an obstacle confronting all of us, wicked and righteous alike, is self-satisfaction, the smug conviction that "I'm okay, you're okay," that whatever flaws one may have are the inevitable lot of human beings. Such spiritual and moral complacency has no necessary relation to one's objective condition. One may be seen by others as a sinner and a criminal, without being at all aware of one's failings. Such a person will never attain *teshuvah*. Similarly, one may come to do *teshuvah* through an awareness of imperfections in himself that are not at all evident to others.

This great stumbling block has been referred to by one sage as "obtuseness of the heart." Obtuseness of the mind is easily recognized as an impairment of cognitive functioning; that of the heart is more insidious, a condition of blocked moral and emotional awareness. Without this prodding awareness, however slight, without some feeling of inadequacy, no amount of intellectual sagacity can change a person's behavior. In many cases, *teshuvah* itself, once underway, gathers steam and produces an "opening of the heart," in which the initial block against the consciousness of one's failings is fully overcome. For the very first crack of awareness leads to a wider, deeper opening, and thus to a stronger response.

These observations hold true for all kinds of people, from

those whose lives have always been far removed from the realm of the sacred and who feel no lack in that area, to those who lead pious lives which they are so satisfied with that they cannot see how far they are from perfection. The initial perception and awakening is, in effect, the first and most inclusive "confession." When a vague feeling of discomfort turns to clear recognition that something is wrong, and when that recognition is expressed in words spoken either to oneself, to God, or to another person, the first step in the process of turning has been taken, the part that relates to one's previous life and character.

The second ingredient in *teshuvah* is referred to as *kabbalah le'atid*—resolve. This step is, in a sense, essentially a continuation of the first, and its force, direction, and coherence are largely determined by the clarity and strength of the initial recognition concerning the past. To feel discomfort and explain it away with a shrug, or any number of verbal equivalents, may not lead to even the *decision* to change, let alone change itself. On the other hand, genuine regret for one's misdeeds and recognition of one's failings do not necessarily lead to the desired outcome either; instead, they can cause a deepening sense of despair and a fatalistic resignation. Rather than promoting positive change, such despondency, regarded in our tradition as one of the most serious afflictions of the soul, can cause one to sink even further. A person may come to feel so degraded, morally, religiously, or otherwise, that he decides to blot out altogether from his consciousness the source of his degradation. Such repression usually occurs when one takes up a life of instinctual pleasures or any of various pursuits designed to dull the senses, temporarily or permanently. It is a flight from depression. Alcohol, drugs, sex, and various forms of "entertainment" may obliterate feelings of discomfort or dissatisfaction, but nothing is solved. Rather, there is a distorted sense of relief from pain and the delusion that one can carry on as before.

Thus remorse alone, however decisive it may be initially, must be accompanied by something else: belief in the possibility of change. In this sense, the principle of *teshuvah*—that no matter what the starting point, no matter how far gone the sinner, penitence is possible—is itself an important source of reawakening and hope. Knowing that the door is always open and that there is a way through it, knowing that there is no irredeemable situation, can itself serve as a goad to *teshuvah*.

It is important to remember that resolutions are not always carried out. Great obstacles lie hidden along the way. Routine and habit, which often create a person's predicament to begin with, do not disappear simply because that person has made up his mind to change. Even though it may not immediately be carried out, the decision is in itself an essential step. As long as it is not mere talk or self-deception (one can deceive oneself as readily as one can others), every positive decision, however small, is important. Indeed, in some cases a person's great turn may appear to be made suddenly, at a sharp angle and at high speed. But usually such a turn is preceded by many less dramatic, less mature steps, small decisions that do not bear fruit, wishes never carried out. When the time comes, all these small moves coalesce into a single movement.

Teshuvah, then, is a universe unto itself, encompassing two apparent opposites: It is, on the one hand, an exceedingly lengthy path with no clear end. Whatever one's starting point, each subsequent moment of change throughout life becomes part of the unfolding of that initial inner resolve to make the turn. On the other hand, *teshuvah* can be seen as a flash of regret and resolution, a sudden insight that change and improvement are needed. These two aspects of *teshuvah* are not contradictory but complementary. When *teshuvah* is seen as a process of complete self-transformation, nothing could be more difficult; yet nothing could be easier than the momentary resolve that sets the process going.

The *ba'al teshuvah* is thus like a person on a journey who at some point decides to change direction. From that point on, his steps will be carrying him toward a different destination. The turn itself is accomplished in a second. Yet the new path, like the one abandoned, is long and arduous.

2

Teshuvah in the Modern World

Though *teshuvah* has always been fundamental to Judaism, far-reaching changes experienced by the Jewish people in recent times have given the process a new dimension. In the past it had a definite human and social meaning as an integral part of Jewish religious life, and to a great extent this is still true. Religious people, too, even the most saintly and scrupulous, can trip and fall into sin. There are many possible causes: an instinctual impulse; a general decline in the level of one's conduct as the result of a weakening of religious motivation; a sudden, wholesale abandonment of the Jewish way of life; or recurrent self-doubt springing from a sense of unfulfilled religious potential. (The latter feeling, in particular, can overcome even individuals considered by others to be paragons of piety.) Whatever the cause, a feeling of regret and a desire to do penitence may follow. Every transgression and experience of failure has its appropriate means of *teshuvah*, from the simple decision to abandon a particular course of misconduct to a struggle for the renewal and elevation of the soul.

Most of what has been written about *teshuvah* is concerned with the various stages of the process: how one is awakened to

8

the necessity of it, when it is appropriate to do it, what attitude is called for, and what specific acts of redress must be performed, from the injunction to return stolen money to instructions regarding physical self-denial and those means of atonement known as *Teshuvat Hakane*.* All this assumes a religious context. When one sinned, stumbled, or went astray, it was as a departure from a pious way of life to which the person and those around him were committed. These kinds of *teshuvah* are still valid, of course, in the religious world; individuals periodically lapse in their observance and try to make amends and return to the Lord. But a new kind of *teshuvah*, quite unlike its predecessors, has made its appearance in the last generation: the *teshuvah* of one completely outside the religious fold, to whom the entire pattern of observance, the yoke of the *mitzvot*, is foreign. The halakhic term that best fits this new phenomenon is "an infant raised among gentiles." This is not to say that *ba'alei teshuvah* of the new variety are subject to all the details of the laws that apply in that case, but that it aptly describes their spiritual state. They are like captives, spiritual captives, among the gentiles, whether the latter be actual non-Jews or Jews who think, speak, and behave like non-Jews. (Even in Israeli society there are many people who think of themselves as Jews, but whose way of life and outlook are indistinguishable, except in language and locale, from those of other peoples.)

The return of the "infant raised among gentiles" is in many ways, even according to *halakhah*, fundamentally different from the *teshuvah* described in the traditional literature. The former, too, is a return, but not to some personal point of departure. Rather, it is a return in a deeper sense, a return of the individual to his people, to his origins, to the crucible in which he was formed, both historically and morally—to God. Judaism and the Jewish people welcome all who wish to come "home," from near and far. But how much greater and more powerful is the act of one who returns to a home he never knew. The person who momentarily goes astray seeks in his *teshuvah* to correct a flaw in the ongoing pattern of his life. The person who comes

---

* A system of ascetic practices and mortifications for the repentant from the Book of Hakane, a medieval kabbalistic work by Rabbi Alkane ben Yeruchem.

to Torah Judaism from outside must make a fundamental change in his way of living and thinking, he must undergo a radical upheaval. What may seem like a quantitative difference between the two kinds of *teshuvah* is in reality a qualitative one.

The latter-day *ba'al teshuvah* enters a new world. The magnitude of the change is not just in the fact that he must now fulfill a certain number of *mitzvot* and cope with a system of specific "ritual requirements." A Jew is indeed subject to many different sacred laws, yet it is not their number but rather their scope—the number of different areas of life on which they impinge—that makes for such an upheaval. To accept Judaism in its entirety is not merely to set aside a certain corner of one's life as a sanctuary, outside the everyday flow of affairs, but to alter deeply that flow itself. More than this, there is a whole new culture to be absorbed, entailing a great deal of learning. Above all, the *ba'al teshuvah* must embrace the subculture of *limud Torah* (study of the Torah), not as a means, but as an end in itself. A culture is more than a set of rules to guide behavior; it is a comprehensive world-view and way of relating to one's fellow human beings. Like all complex cultures, Jewish culture does not spell everything out literally, but leaves much to inference. A culture's strength lies not only in what it says, but also in what it chooses not to say, and this too must be learned.

This world, with all its difficulties and charms, is the one the modern *ba'al teshuvah* enters. Some get acquainted with it ahead of time through reading; others have looked at it, often with hostility, from the outside. But the knowledge acquired as a participant is not only deeper than, but also essentially different from, that of an observer. The difference between "I am praying" and "he is praying" is not merely a matter of viewpoint or of substituting one pronoun for another; it denotes an altogether different experience. Another's prayers, another's faith, are "phenomena" that I see and judge according to my own criteria. My prayers, my faith, the *mitzvot* I fulfill, spring from my personal involvement and connection. The transition from the status of observer to that of participant does not take place all at once; in fact, it may be quite prolonged, involving many stages. Yet every one of these stages entails a change in substance, not just form.

There is thus a strong element of internal struggle in modern-day *teshuvah*. The *teshuvah* done by one who has never left the Jewish fold is also the result of a struggle: between temptation—instinct, inertia, habit—and awareness. The leap to *teshuvah* takes place at the point where awareness somehow overcomes temptation. The way is then clear, and the power available, to change direction. In the *teshuvah* done nowadays by people new to the Jewish frame of reference, the internal struggle centers on the ability to make the transition from one cultural, experiential world to another. The basic difficulty is in the essential change in one's pattern of relating, a change more difficult than any other practical or personal problems that may arise.

It has always been said that smooth continuity was not to be expected in the process of *teshuvah*, that at some point a leap would have to be taken from one realm to another. The exodus from Egypt, considered the archetype of spiritual liberation, takes place in two stages: the moment of hesitation and the moment of release. The Jewish people hesitate at the shore of the Red Sea, then, suddenly, Nahshon leaps into the deep water. In other words, even with the help of numerous miracles and the pressure of a cruel enemy in hot pursuit, a crucial pause halts the steady onward march. One runs up against a barrier that cannot be traversed except by making a bold decision, taking a chance, and jumping. Such hurdles are always part of *teshuvah*, but they are immeasurably more difficult when, as in our time, *teshuvah* is a matter of summoning the strength to leave one world for another.

In this connection it is worth recalling a rule that applies in the spiritual as much as in the physical realm: passage from one kind of environment to another may involve hundreds or thousands of little steps, but there comes a certain moment of categorical change, a moment unlike any that came before or any that are to follow. One can pace up and down the shore or wade about in the shallows for a long time, even a lifetime, contemplating swimming, but until one takes the plunge, one is not swimming. One cannot get swimming experience without giving up the security of treading on solid ground, without actually lifting one's feet, even before there is absolute certainty that one can stay afloat. Thus it is in every such transition; there is a moment of risk, of uncertainty, every time a plane takes off or lands.

Entering the world of Judaism is like entering a different medium, and one who would experience that medium must at some point make a decision for change. That is not to say that a sudden leap is by itself appropriate; leaping before one is ready to make the transition is dangerous and sometimes damaging. But prolonged theoretical exercises and circumambulations, aimed at preparation and gradual adjustment, must at some point culminate in a jump from old to new values and new ways of thinking if one is to cross into the new world. Sometimes it happens that one takes the final step, not deliberately, but helped along by circumstances, as when a person hesitating over whether to jump into the water accidentally falls in. Subjectively, there is little difference between the two situations, the one in which all the impetus comes from within and the one in which there are also some compelling external factors. In both cases there is bound to be an element of shock, a sudden loss of stability. Before a new equilibrium can be achieved, the old one must be abandoned; the two cannot be maintained simultaneously.

Undoubtedly there are cases in which the transition is instantaneous, unambiguous, and irreversible, in which one enters the world of Judaism and feels immediately at home, as if he had never been anywhere else. But one does not necessarily make a single decision or a single abrupt leap and thereby become a new person; often a lengthy process is required. Yet even in such cases a crucial difference distinguishes the person who has not made a decision to change from the one who has already made the move, however briefly or partially. One who has managed to cross over to the new world has undergone an experience of inestimable importance that cannot be taken away from him: he now knows that it is *possible* for him to accomplish this change. For above all the other difficulties, uncertainties, and misgivings, both practical and intellectual, a great question looms: can this thing really be done? Can I really imagine myself on the other side, in the world of Judaism? But once the leap is made, however briefly, this essential question is answered, just as it is for the would-be swimmer who pushes off for the first time or for the aspiring flier on his first flight. No doubt the second time is difficult, too, and turning the initial experiment into an ongoing way of life even more so; but it is now clear that it can be done. The difficulties now are of a different kind: matters of detail, of practicality rather than principle, of *zil gemor*—going on to study the ramifications of a step already taken.

Another common aspect of *teshuvah* concerns one of its most essential, and paradoxical, components. On the one hand, *teshuvah* entails a break with the past, fixing a cut-off point that divides one's life into a "before" and an "after." Indeed, the ability to atone for and rectify one's mistakes rests on the assumption that such a break is possible, that *teshuvah* results in the creation of a completely new being. The past is severed from the present; one's former self becomes a stranger or ceases to exist. Or, as the Sages put it, the sinner one dies and passes from this world; the penitent self is a new creature. *Teshuvah* is thus a kind of spiritual death and rebirth.

On the other hand, it is the past that motivates *teshuvah* and gives it its specific character. The saying of the Sages that "in the place where *ba'alei teshuvah* stand, even saints cannot stand" is explained by the Zohar to mean that *ba'alei teshuvah* "draw out" the Holy One, blessed be He, "with greater force." In the course of *teshuvah*, they develop a religious tension that is far stronger than that found among those who move along the same path throughout their lives. To use a simile of the Sages, it is only the damming up of a river that makes its power evident. It is the very distance of the *ba'al teshuvah* from holiness in his former life that lends force to his present yearning. The measured pace of one whose whole life is lived uprightly becomes a frenzied rush in the case of the *ba'al teshuvah*, who is driven by a sense of lack to strive for that which has been "lost." In *teshuvah*, these two apparently contradictory movements—the break with the past and the thrust provided by it—must both be given expression. The *ba'al teshuvah* must be, in some ways, like a "newborn babe," but he cannot feel completely so. He must be reborn, paradoxically, as a mature adult.

The greatest difficulty the modern *ba'al teshuvah* is likely to face arises when he tries to ignore his past altogether. (I shall discuss this at greater length in Chapter 9.) Doing so can have some apparent benefits, but also carries with it the dangers of self-satisfaction, smugness, and impatience with the difficulties of others. One becomes callous and insensitive, losing sight of the fact that people differ and that those who are different are not necessarily worse. It is only by remembering one's own past, by seeing the past as an integral part of one's life, that one can make the proper assessments. Though the *ba'al teshuvah* may now find himself in a "different world," he must remember that he was not always there and that he is still responsible for what came before. He is thus saved from two opposing pitfalls: excessive self-deprecation, to the point of self-destructiveness, and excessive self-esteem. The modern *ba'al teshuvah* can, of course, claim that his past transgressions were not his personal failure or his succumbing to temptation, but rather the fault of his parents, the environment in which he grew up, or his people. While such a claim has some validity, it should not altogether replace one's regrets.

In fact, there is no way to escape the past and be reborn completely anew. On the contrary, even one who has undergone the most extreme change, who has turned his values and beliefs completely upside down, does not generally become a different kind of person than he was. Character and personality usually remain stable despite great changes in one's way of life; if they were flawed before, they are likely to remain so. Thus one who looks upon *teshuvah* as a panacea for personal problems is bound to be disappointed. Weaknesses may be dressed up in the garb of piety, but they remain weaknesses. That is not to say that imperfections cannot be corrected, but that they can be corrected only when they are consciously and directly addressed. One can and must overcome discouragement and gloom, rashness and arrogance, but only by making a strenuous effort to do so. "Esau's master," as the ancients called the evil impulse, is, according to the Sages, revealed in two ways: Sometimes it is like a robber, open and violent. Sometimes it is like a scholar who is full of wisdom and understanding, psychological sensitivity, and even ethical and religious fervor, all of which can be clever obstacles on the path toward the good. These obstacles can take the form of imposing demands so high that few people can realize them, or of dwelling on spiritual problems so complex that they cannot be resolved. We must be wary of both dangers.

Thus, even after his great spiritual about-face, the modern *ba'al teshuvah* must come back to himself, to scrutinize what has really changed, to see whether the changes that have taken place are deep-seated or merely on the surface. No less than before, he must use his awareness of his past failings as a goad to push him onward. It is not a matter of breast-beating but of an ongoing self-evaluation.

— 3 —

All or Nothing: The False Dilemma

A person still hesitantly groping his way toward *teshuvah* may well find his life filled with contradiction and torn between conflicting aims. By the very nature of things, the seeker lives in a complex, imperfect world. Once his resolve in favor of *teshuvah* is complete, this confused state undergoes a dramatic change. Arriving at such a resolve, however, often seems to entail a painful dilemma: choosing between an absolute commitment to a wholly Jewish way of life and the complete rejection of such a life.

One who opts for the path of *teshuvah* knows that Judaism can never again be a mere hobby for him, something to take up whenever it amuses him to do so, then to lay aside. More than this, Judaism itself puts emphasis, both in thought and practice, on its own inclusiveness. It asks to be seen not just as a random assortment of unrelated beliefs and observances, but as an integral whole, however complex. To the *ba'al teshuvah*, undertaking only part of what Judaism demands seems like self-deception, a kind of trick played on the Creator of the universe and oneself. "If I am really sincere," he says to himself, "I must stop playing games and picking and choosing. I must take the whole thing upon myself and give myself over to it, body and soul." But a move of such finality is far from easy; long-established habits, views, friendships, and work patterns all get in the way. No uniform pattern of obstacles confronts all would-be *ba'alei teshuvah*, but for most, Judaism poses serious problems. No doubt, situations exist in which one can freely choose, in which it is possible for one to reorder all at once the circumstances and patterns of one's life; but such situations are few, rare conjunctions of favorable conditions within and without. For most of us, such radical change is not a simple matter. The old involvements and patterns cause conflict, embarrassment, even revulsion. And fighting all these counterforces at once can seem overwhelming.

The contradiction between the desire for *teshuvah* and the many obstacles blocking the way to it leaves the prospective *ba'al teshuvah* hanging, uncertain as to what direction his life is to take. To do everything seems an unreachable goal; to do less seems unworthy and dishonest. The only apparent alternative, then, if one is to be honest with oneself and with God, is to do nothing, or at least to wait until the right moment, the moment of grace, arrives.

The spiritual and intellectual need to make some final, clear-cut choice of path is a great stumbling block for many, particularly the more sensitive and thoughtful. For while the dilemma is real, the notion that it must be resolved all at once, in so final and unequivocal a way, is mistaken and dangerous. A choice between "all or nothing" is inappropriate, in terms both of the essential character of Judaism itself and of any sort of authentic personal relationship to it. True, one of the cardinal principles of Judaism is that the *mitzvot* are all of a piece, parts of a single whole that is in its essence complete, the details being knit together into a unified fabric. Yet the inner connectedness of the *mitzvot* has another significance; just as the failure to perform a single *mitzvah* diminishes the whole, each *mitzvah* in a sense *includes* the whole. In the prayer "For the Unification," recited before the performance of many *mitzvot*, one prays "to fulfill the *mitzvah* of . . . in all its particulars, and the 613 *mitzvot* that depend upon it." All 613 are in a sense compressed into each individual *mitzvah*.

The oneness of the *mitzvot* should not be viewed as the mechanical construction of diverse elements for the sake of a common higher purpose, but rather as a unity similar to that of nature itself. Each part of creation draws nourishment from all the other parts, and thus enfolds into itself something of their essence.

The all-encompassing character of each *mitzvah* is a multifaceted idea, treated on a number of levels of interpretation, from the mystical and esoteric to the *halakhic* and pragmatic. Just as the deliberate violation of a single *mitzvah* is to be regarded, in a sense, as an act of rebellion against Divine authority in general, so too can the acceptance and fulfillment of a single *mitzvah* be seen as an acceptance of the fundamental, primary meaning of the *mitzvot* in general, an acceptance of the yoke of the Kingdom of Heaven. The fulfillment of one *mitzvah* is thus tantamount to the recognition of the basic principle of the Divine-human connection and all that it signifies. However isolated, it is an act fraught with significance. This view is in accord with that of *halakhah* itself: the failure to fulfill a given *mitzvah*, for whatever reason, does not exempt one from the fulfillment of other *mitzvot*. For example, one who actively violates *Shabbat* is not thereby relieved of the duty of lighting *Shabbat* candles.

Alongside the general obligation to fulfill the *mitzvot* there is a particular obligation attached to each individual *mitzvah*, and the one has no bearing on the other. A person who, through neglect, develops a malady in one part of his body, need not, for the sake of consistency, neglect the other parts as well. So it is with the *mitzvot*.

The question of "all or nothing" is also invalid from a human, personal point of view. Though the *ba'al teshuvah* may wish to see himself as one reborn and to begin his spiritual life with a sense of wholeness, it is important for him to recognize that even in spiritual rebirth it is not possible to take on everything at once. The People of Israel, in accepting the Torah, did not receive it all at one time. Rather, the process was a protracted one, from the early preparatory stage of the seven

Noahide laws to the acceptance of additional *mitzvot* in Egypt, at Marah, and at Sinai, to the full revelation there that followed. Similarly, a child raised to be an observant Jew takes upon itself the full yoke of the *mitzvot* only after long preparation: years of training and the gradual, step-by-step assumption of responsibility according to its intellectual readiness and practical capacity.

The essential point is that living beings do not undergo sudden, complete transformations. The caterpillar does not become a butterfly in a single act but as a result of a gradual process, governed by certain laws. Within this process there appears to be a series of jumps between distinct stages, and these the *ba'al teshuvah* also must make from time to time. But these transitions, too, are neither as quick nor as sharp as they appear.

Sudden entry into the world of Jewish religious life is a rare phenomenon for the simple reason that these changes are highly complex. The acceptance of Judaism is not a matter of one-time affirmations or moments of revelation. Such transitory experiences can be important as turning points, but in Judaism they can serve only as the starting point of a very long journey. It must be remembered that Judaism is a complicated mixture of cultural elements in which belief and practice are closely intertwined. Without the combination of these elements, Judaism is incomplete. This is the reason for the prolonged educational process that must be undergone by the Jewish people in its history and by each individual Jew. It is also why the *ba'al teshuvah* is likely to find himself engaged for an extended period in such an educational process. Instead of seeing the intermediate stages as signs of insincerity and ambivalence, as evidence that he is fooling God and himself, he must learn to see them as steps in this process of education.

To be sure, the education of an adult, whose personal universe is already well-defined, differs from the training of a child. Problems that are beyond the child's mental grasp or physical ability may seem quite simple to the adult. Conversely, matters that pose no problem to the innocent, untainted mind of the child may present the adult with serious difficulties.

The problems of the *ba'al teshuvah* are likely to be distinctive, and they are also bound to differ from one person to another. Things that seem fundamental or intolerable to one person may be inconsequential to another. For one person, questions of identity and peer group may be decisive, while for another, the crux will be issues of principle. As in other matters, there is no single path all can follow. Nonetheless, there is a common denominator: recognition that the achievement of faith and, beyond that, a fully Jewish life is no small matter and that many transitional stages will be required to attain them. None of these stages is an end in itself, but at the same time no stage is merely a sham or false front.

In a way, the *ba'al teshuvah* should regard himself as though he were about to undertake to solve a complicated mathematical problem, one that can be solved only by some rare flash of intuition or to which there is a (likewise rare) single, unambiguous solution, reachable through a series of intermediate steps. No one of these is sufficient in itself to solve the problem, and in many cases the intermediate solution leaves the greater part of the problem obscure. Nevertheless, each fragment of a solution represents an advance toward the ultimate goal.

This is not to say that the graduated path to Judaism represents a simple process either. The path is strewn with difficulties and obstacles the seeker must be aware of. The first is the lack of wholeness one feels en route. When one is already living a fully Jewish life, the various parts of one's existence—one's network of associations, identity, thoughts, and actions—form a coherent whole. But one in transition, passing from stage to stage, necessarily becomes entangled in contradictions. His identity is blurred and his relations with the world around him are confused. The very awareness of these contradictions is baffling and painful, sometimes to the point of despair. The world left behind now seems alien and inhospitable, but the *ba'al teshuvah* has not yet experienced the liberating sense of having reached the new world. On the other hand, the knowledge that this is just a passing phase can be reassuring, and its very discomfort can serve as a goad to press on until a new, relatively stable equilibrium is reached.

Another problem, deeper and more dangerous, is the tendency of some who begin the process of *teshuvah* to remain forever en route and never reach any definite destination. The perpetuation of the transitory state leads to aimlessness and a confused self-image; but more than this, it is contrary to the very meaning of the transition process. The sole justification for living in a state of inner contradiction is that this state is one of transition and transformation. The transition process may be prolonged, for, like the resolution of other dilemmas in life, it requires self-education and change. But the undertaking loses its theological and moral meaning when the original goal, that of embracing Judaism in its totality, is lost sight of. In the early stages that goal may seem quite remote and forbidding, but without it, why set out? In this sense, an all-or-nothing decision *is* vital; one's commitment to the ultimate aim must be absolute, however long and tortuous the way leading there may be.

The decisive point in the turn to Judaism is not the initial awakening, which can be seen merely as a response to a call. It is, rather, the inward affirmation of "we shall do and we shall obey"*—the decision to address one's life to the realization of this commitment—that makes the turn real. Rather than waiting for an opportune time to make the change all at once—something that may never come along—it is better to change one's life gradually, by stages, according to one's inner capacity and outward circumstances. But this does not lessen the importance of making a firm decision at the outset. There is a crucial moment in which one "receives the Torah," with all its contents, both general and specific. It is then that one sets out on the path, toward the realization of one's resolve. Some are able to achieve this relatively easily, passing as if by magic from one world to the other, and encountering few obstacles or difficulties. But for most it is a complex, long drawn-out process, fraught with tribulations. And again the question that must be asked is not, "Must I do all or nothing?" but rather, "What beginning can I make that will facilitate eventually reaching the goal of doing all?"

---

* Exodus 24:7.

4

Where to Begin?

Taking upon oneself the yoke of the Torah and the *mitzvot* is by no means an easy task. Becoming "religious" in the Jewish sense means not only acquiring a propensity for the sort of numinous feelings experienced in a house of worship; it means the adoption of a distinct and all-pervasive way of life. One's education, environment, and relation to that environment all figure prominently in the ease or difficulty of taking such a step. But in no case is it an easy step to take.

Some can make the leap all at once, and various kinds of *yeshivot* and institutions can facilitate it. Those who are younger and those less encumbered with familial and professional ties will find the transition easier to make. With others, the way to Judaism can be greatly protracted, plagued by doubts and reversals and only gradually yielding a certain stability.

Those who make the journey slowly and reluctantly are troubled by questions of all kinds, but early on they confront a question of special importance: Where to begin? How does one take the first practical step? Even when the prospective *ba'al teshuvah* feels ready to take on everything, it is in the nature of lengthy odysseys that they be made in a series of small steps that only much later coalesce into a meaningful whole. As in other human endeavors, there are no hard and fast rules here. Every individual has good and bad sides, particular problems and inhibitions. Still, certain limited generalizations can be made, and they can provide some guidance.

First, the prospective *ba'al teshuvah* should not try to impose upon himself in advance a rigid plan or list of priorities. The fact of having begun the process is more important than the particular things one begins with. Second, one's initial observances should be in an area that is close to the heart, for which one already has a particular affinity, and not of the sort one would have to force oneself to undertake. The Sages advise us to single out certain *mitzvot* for special care and devotion; indeed, most observant Jews do feel a special closeness to, and derive particular satisfaction from, a few *mitzvot*. It is with these *mitzvot* rather than others that it is best to begin. Third, whatever observances are chosen, they should be undertaken with the intention of keeping them indefinitely. In any kind of worthy endeavor, failure is to be expected and should be taken in stride. In the case of the *mitzvot*, however, it is important to at least begin with a sense of permanent commitment. This applies even if the initial observance is a relatively minor one. When a person takes on an obligation that he does not expect to be able to fulfill indefinitely, he undermines his own sense of seriousness about the undertaking and causes himself additional crises of commitment.

It is best from both a religious and a psychological point of view to begin with the negative precepts—avoiding what is forbidden—rather than with the burden of positive obligations. The inner effort involved in refraining from many of the prohibitions is small compared with their halakhic gravity. It is also small compared with the effort involved in positive observance: the prohibitions call for self-restraint and overcoming habits but not for daily, conscious activity.

The need to refrain from things one has long been accustomed to requires a lengthy process of adjustment. One who is not used to *Shabbat* observance will continue for some time to feel uncomfortable with what seem like all-pervasive restrictions; he will continue, too, to violate these restrictions unintentionally, out of sheer force of habit, only realizing afterward what he has done. For example, he will not easily get used to not turning on and off lights and other electrical appliances. It takes time for this restriction to become second nature, and all the more so with prohibitions against activities that are inherently pleasurable. Thus smokers who refrain from tobacco for a full twenty-four hours are likely to experience physical discomfort. Once the observance of *Shabbat* becomes habitual, however, the very atmosphere of the day has the effect of blocking conflicting mental and physical habits, even for a person not raised on such observance. The same holds true for sexual abstinence during the part of the menstrual cycle when marital relations are forbidden. The power of habit and attraction may initially make such abstinence difficult, but it becomes easier as one progressively takes upon oneself the overall framework of observance.

At times it seems to the "outsider" that observance comes easily to his religious acquaintances, that it is fraught with privation only for him. In fact, even people who grow up in observant families have their difficulties. Everyone feels desire, and has trouble harnessing it to the pursuit of noble ends. The struggle to do so must be unremitting, and setbacks are not uncommon. It is true that proper habits can make the struggle easier, but rarely can temptation be eliminated altogether.

Seen in this light, a particularly easy area of negative observance to begin with is that concerning food (see Chapter 19). In Israel and other countries with large Jewish communities, kosher food is readily obtainable and the food problem is easily solved. Kashering a kitchen is something that anyone can do; and it is easier to give up certain foods and eating habits than other proscribed things. A certain sense of beneficial self-purification may even ensue.

The positive observances, too, are appropriate for beginners to different degrees. One *mitzvah* that often starts *ba'alei teshuvah* on their way is quite fundamental: *talmud Torah*, the study of Torah (see Chapter 14). Regular study—and the regularity is important even if the study be infrequent or for brief periods of time—can serve as an impetus to further progress. It is important, though not absolutely necessary, that this *mitzvah* be performed in the right company; when people study together, they help and reinforce each other. Another such *mitz-*

vah, one which is conducive to further observance provided the beginner is temperamentally open to it, is regular prayer, even if only once a week. This *mitzvah* also is relatively easy to fulfill.

For many people, one of the most difficult aspects of moving from one world to another is the self-consciousness caused by the unavoidable public aspects of the process. Often one feels a hesitancy or tentativeness about religious commitment that one is reluctant to display. Those who feel such anxiety should begin with "private" observances, those that can be performed without others knowing about them. Later one can take up family observances; after that, communal ones, those involving public identification. Private prayer, solitary donning of *tefillin*, lighting *Shabbat* candles at home—all these are easy ways to begin. Once a certain amount of self-confidence has been built up, more public changes in one's way of life can be undertaken.

To repeat, everyone progresses at a different pace. There are those whose temperament or way of life makes it easier for them to change quickly, while others need much more time to cover the same distance, and they do so with greater inner uncertainty. It is important to remember that each positive precept fulfilled, each transgression avoided, is in itself an achievement. The first step is never sufficient, but even the longest journey must begin somewhere.

— 5 —

Actions and Intentions

When it comes to the practical details of what, when, and how, there is no lack of guidance to the many *mitzvot* incumbent upon a Jew. For the uninitiated, finding the right books and understanding their idiom may prove difficult. Like other technical skills, the performance of the *mitzvot* explained using technical vocabulary. Some books try to help the reader with diagrams and pictures, but these too can pose difficulties for the novice. In most cases, and particularly when it comes to the details of everyday observance, it is best to rely on the example of a more experienced practitioner, and to consult books later on, either for the sake of review or to explore the varieties of custom. But one way or another, practical guidance is available.

What is not so readily available is guidance to the inner dimension of the *mitzvot*, the dimension of thought and inner experience. Of course, such matters are not as uniform or clear cut: the inward differences between people are even greater than their outward differences; thoughts or inner experiences are not easily expressed; and objective performance is no reliable indicator of subjective intent. From a halakhic point of view, the act alone is generally sufficient ("*mitzvot* do not require intent"), but even here matters are not as simple as they may seem. A minimum motivation and attention are required for the fulfillment of most *mitzvot*. Furthermore, that which, after the fact, is considered sufficient to have "discharged one's obligation" (so that repetition is unnecessary), differs greatly from that which is expected from the outset. The benedictions accompanying most positive *mitzvot* affirm one's intention to carry them out *because* they are *mitzvot*. Beyond this, most of the liturgical traditions append fixed (if not obligatory) formulas—beginning with *leshem yihud*, "For the sake of the Unification"—further elaborating the doer's sacred intent in performing the *mitzvah*.

The saying in the Zohar that "without awe and love, [the study of] Torah and [the performance of] *mitzvot* do not reach heaven" expresses the difference between routine mechanical acts and those in which the soul is involved. The act is something objective; regardless of intent, it makes a real difference whether the act is good or bad. A deed that in context has good effects remains good whether or not the doer intended it so in the depths of his soul. But this yardstick applies only to the relation between the deed and its outer context. There is also another yardstick: just as forced transgressions do not count and accidental misdeeds are judged less harshly, so too is only the most meager value attached to *mitzvot* done unintentionally, unwittingly, or mechanically. To be sure, intentions *alone* accomplish nothing; they only become significant in relation to the actions they lead to. (The *mitzvot* of the heart, such as the love and fear of God, are exceptions.) By the same token, a misdeed committed with the best of intentions remains a misdeed. There is thus a complex interconnection—a complementary relationship—between the act of the *mitzvah*, with all its practical details, and the intention behind it.

The more seriously one takes the *mitzvot* and the greater the weight one gives to their inward dimension, the more one will raise questions of how and why, questions of essence. In a sense, the entire Torah can be seen as a set of explanations for the *mitzvot*, from the elucidation of how they are to be carried out to the study of their manifold meanings on a variety of planes. The great principle of "we shall do and we shall hear"

refers not only to the need to obey and the willingness to do
so without hesitation; the "we shall do" aspect of a given *mitzvah* is essentially quite simple and easily attainable, whereas the
"we shall hear" part is almost infinite, just as the Torah itself
is "broader than the earth" and inexhaustible. In the study of
Torah one can draw a distinction (of practical rather than intellectual consequence) between investigation that is directly
related to the performance of the *mitzvah* at hand, and that
which is unrelated. In other words, each *mitzvah* is expostulated
according to commentary and rabbinic tradition (*midrash halakhah*) concerning the Torah-text, on the one hand, and according to the details of what, when, and how (practical *halakhah*), on the other. But there is yet a third body of inquiry:
concerning *kavannah* (intention), that which gives subjective
meaning to the *mitzvah* in the mind of the doer at the moment
when he carries it out.

One of the most basic kinds of *kavannah* is the awareness
that one is about to perform a *mitzvah*, to fulfill the will of the
Creator. Such *kavannah* arises from the recognition that the
mitzvah is a vehicle for the relationship between human beings
and the Divine. The heartfelt desire for transcendence, for some
kind of contact with the Holy One, blessed be He, is the inner
expression of the human soul, the very essence of humanness.
This aspiration, which grows ever stronger as one's inner stature grows, can never be fully realized, for with spiritual growth
and the deepening of knowledge comes ever clearer recognition
of the unbridgeable chasm between oneself and the infinite.
Ordinary satisfactions are attained easily enough, but to attain
something higher, beyond normal human limitations, is possible only through Divine grace. The *mitzvah*, then, is essentially just a line connecting heaven and earth, a sort of epistle
from on high, a finger extended in order to be grasped. Its decisive importance lies not in its content or efficacy, be it material or spiritual, but in the fact that it constitutes a point of
contact with the Divine. Performing a *mitzvah* means, above
all, making such contact. God's will can be realized only
through a connection with Him, be it just in the moment of
the sacred act. Herein lies the general intent or *kavannah* of all
the *mitzvot*, the positive and the negative, those concerned with
behavior and those concerned with belief. Here too we find the

primary determinants of the quality of the performance of a given *mitzvah:* the love and fear of God.

For each *mitzvah* there are also various levels and types of specific *kavannah*. There is, for exmple, the mystical *kavannah*, such as those embodied in the meditative formulas that appear in certain prayerbooks. These formulas (also called *kavannot*) may either be incorporated into the liturgy ("For the sake of the Unification, etc.") or stand alone. In fact, several prayerbooks are oriented entirely in this direction. Another type of *kavannah* is based on the *symbolic* meaning imputed to the various *mitzvot* by rabbinic tradition. Both mystical and symbolic *kavannot* are essentially forms of communion with the Divine, but are active and affective rather than intellectual or abstract. The meditation lends the performance of the *mitzvah*, the outward physical act, a depth and warmth of feeling and a spiritual exaltation.

In addition, there are very personal *kavannot*, fashioned by each individual out of his own store of meanings and the symbolic associations he has with particular *mitzvot*. Great care must be taken in this regard, especially by those insufficiently schooled in Jewish sources and inexperienced in observance. Such people can unwittingly fall prey to misconceptions and distortions. They may even be driven by their mistaken notions to do things quite contrary to Judaism. It is thus best, in focusing one's thoughts on the performance of a *mitzvah*, to ground them in the words of the Torah and the Sages.

The question of the *kavannot* that should accompany the performance of *mitzvot* is in itself a big subject. Let us then focus on two particular *mitzvot*; both occur regularly, and both contain an inner content that can, if one is aware of it, make the act more meaningful.

The *mitzvah* of donning *tefillin* every weekday morning is one of the positive commandments incumbent only on men. It is forbidden to don *tefillin* on *Shabbat* and on the festivals. As to *Hol Hamo'ed*, views differ: in *Eretz Yisrael tefillin* are not worn, while in the Diaspora they are put on only by those who observe the Ashkenazic rite. Though the *mitzvah* in itself is simple—four passages from the Torah, inscribed inside leather boxes, are placed on the left arm and the head—the details are quite complex, concerning how the *tefillin* are to be made and how they are to be put on. Each detail has a specific meaning and purpose, and the entire teaching could fill several volumes. Because of the careful exactitude required in the making of the *tefillin* and the great importance of the craftsman's intent, a meticulously, reverently made pair of *tefillin* is a prized possession. The *mitzvah* of *tefillin* is also one of the few that, because of disagreement among the authorities, may actually be observed in more than one way by the same person. Thus, it is the custom of many Hasidim and others to put on two pairs of *tefillin* every day, one of the type prescribed by Rashi and one of the type prescribed by Rabbeinu Tam. (The Sephardim put them on together, the Ashkenazim one after the other.) And there are even those who don four pairs.

For many centuries, apparently since the end of the Amoraic period, the *mitzvah* of *tefillin* has been linked with *tefillah* (prayer) or, more precisely, with *shaharit* (the morning service). Since the obligation to don *tefillin* applies only during the daytime, and since this *mitzvah* is itself mentioned in the morning recitation of the *Shema* (Deuteronomy 6:11), the joining of the two is natural. Nevertheless, the connection is not an inherent one: the *mitzvah* of donning *tefillin* can be fulfilled anytime during the daylight hours, even when one is not engaged in prayer. This fact is of some practical significance, since it is not always possible to put them on at the usual time. The *mitzvah* can be fulfilled by simply donning the *tefillin* and immediately taking them off again. Here the inner meaning of the act must be considered. *Tefillin* are not appurtenances of prayer but articles of apparel that symbolize Jewish distinctiveness. On the one hand, they are intended to remind us of our obligation to God; on the other, they signify our special standing in His eyes, our chosenness. These two functions complement one another; the responsibility and the glory go together. Thus both are reflected in the details of *tefillin* observance, in the very construction of the *tefillin* themselves, as well as in the four scriptural passages they contain. In this sense, *tefillin* are like a uniform, the wearing of which is an expression of submission and discipline, and at the same time of authority and dignity.

The most prominent feature of the armpiece is the inward-pointing box—"a sign to you and not to others," in the words of the Sages—representing the acceptance of responsibility. The winding of the strap around the arm, the fingers, and the hand, tied, finally, in the palm, symbolizes a pledge of obedience, an acceptance of "the yoke of the Kingdom of Heaven." Just as one binds the *tefillin* on his hand and close to his heart, so too does he "bind" his hand and heart to God's service. The head-piece, placed at the top of the forehead, is primarily a sign to others, connected by the Sages with the verse, "All the people of the land shall see that you are called by God's Name" (Deuteronomy 28:10). This piece is a prince's crown, the treasure of a treasured people.

One can discern the forms of several Hebrew letters when the straps of the *tefillin* are in place: the double *shin* engraved in the head box, the *dalet* (single or double, according to custom) in the knot of the head strap, and the *yod* on the hand piece. Together, these three letters from *Shaddai*, one of the Divine names. The same name is suggested by the configuration of the strap bound around the hand. *Shaddai* is a name with a double meaning: limitless power, but also blessing, the flow of fruitful life. The donning of *tefillin* is thus an act rich with the manifold meanings of "He who crowns Israel with glory," the glory of bondage of the Creator. As the poet said, "None but the servant of the Lord is free."

Another *mitzvah* passed on since ancient times is that of lighting *Shabbat* and festival candles. This *mitzvah*, one of seven enacted on the authority of the Scribes, may have derived from entirely practical considerations: to provide sufficient light to enjoy a restful and refreshing evening meal. The *mitzvah* of candle-lighting is incumbent on everyone who eats or sleeps alone (including single men), though within the family it is the wife's duty. The Talmud already alludes to a variety of explanations for this, and much has been written about the subject through the ages. It has become customary for women to recite special prayers, composed in any of several languages, just before or just after lighting the candles. These prayers expand on the content of the *mitzvah*.

Again, the halakhic framework for this practice is quite simple, though there is much disagreement about the details. In many places the custom is for a girl to begin lighting one candle at age three or five, as soon as she can say the benediction. Married women, on the other hand, light at least two candles—first, because of the generally dual character of the symbolism of *Shabbat*, and, second, because the candles represent the nuclear family, which is based on the dyad of husband and wife. Many women make it a practice to light as many candles as there are members of the household, while others always light seven, in honor of *Shabbat*. Another custom, which has become widespread and assumed obligatory status, is for a married woman who *forgets* once to light *Shabbat* candles to light an extra candle every week for the rest of her life. (This does not apply where the omission was unavoidable.)

Candle-lighting is done at a set time, which varies from week to week and place to place. It may be done early, as early as noon on Friday, but not later than the set time. In most places the time is customarily fixed at eighteen minutes before sunset, which in turn is the time of *kenissat haShabbat* (the "entrance" of *Shabbat*). During this interval, others in the household are still permitted to finish various tasks essential to preparation for *Shabbat*, while for the woman (or man) who has lit candles, *melakhah* (work) is no longer allowed. Since saying the blessing over the candles is tantamount to "taking on" *Shabbat*, it is customary to do the lighting, cover one's eyes with one's hands while reciting the benediction, then uncover the eyes and look at the candles. It is while the eyes are covered that personal prayers and *kavannot* are said.

As I have indicated, there is much rabbinic discussion of the connection between women's role and the *mitzvah* of lighting candles. The act is seen as one of *tikun olam*, "repairing the world" and illuminating it. Furthermore, *Shabbat* itself, and the Sabbath night in particular, are seen as inherently related to the role and nature of women. The night of *Shabbat* is the time of the exaltation of the *Shekhinah*—God's indwelling Presence in the world. The *Shekhinah* grows stronger on *Shabbat*, its light is more evident, and it turns routine household activities such as eating, drinking, and sleeping into sacred acts. Woman is the eternal symbol of the *Shekhinah*. The *Shabbat* hymns, such as *Lekha Dodi*; the *Shabbat* evening service; *Kiddush*; and the laudatory passage from Proverbs, "A Woman of Valor," recited at the Friday night table, are all replete with imagery linking *Shabbat*, the *Shekhinah*, and women. Each verse and each custom enfolds and unfolds additional levels of association.

The lighting of the candles is not only the first act of welcoming *Shabbat*, in which the members of the household receive its sanctity into their midst; it also expresses the essence of *Shabbat* itself, the penetration of the light of this special day into mundane reality. For, on the surface, this day is no different from any other; the material context of our lives is outwardly unchanged. Yet it is possible to illuminate this outward reality in a way that gives everything about it a different character and meaning. This is the sense of the lines we sing in honor of the *Shekhinah/Shabbat/* the bride:

> *Thy light has come;*
> *Arise, O my light;*
> *The glory of the Lord*
> *Is revealed upon thee.*

As exemplified in these two areas of Jewish life (*tefillin* and candle-lighting), the actual physical performance is only a part of the totality of any *mitzvah*. It is not enough to perform the required action mechanically; one has to do it with a wholeness of spiritual awareness. Conditioned habit is only one of the impediments on this path. There are also times when one gets tired, either simple physical tiredness or spiritual weariness. In addition, many well-intended acts are done under pressure, in haste, or in conditions that distract the heart. If one tries to maintain a high spiritual poise all the time, one soon discovers that it involves a tremendous effort, and is not always possible. Furthermore, it may frequently be appropriate for a person, even one of high spiritual sensitivity, to accept the blessedness of routine, the doing for its own sake, in thoughtless simplicity and purity of heart, as an intrinsic part of the fabric of life. Generally speaking, the tension between deed and intention, between times of inspiration and times of practical action, is also a part of the spiritual way in which a Jewish personality is formed.

6

Lapses and Crises

It is not unusual for the *ba'al teshuvah* to find himself in a state of spiritual crisis, resulting from either an inner sense of inadequacy or some external cause, most commonly the discovery that he has in some way strayed from the straight and narrow path. Though it may seem to him that he has long since mastered a particular difficulty—avoiding a certain transgression or maintaining a certain pattern of positive observance—pressures may arise that cause him to regress. Such pressures may be social or familial in nature, or they may have an obscure origin. The lapse in behavior, in turn, leads to a sense of crisis that may be much farther-reaching than the failing that brought it about.

Such spiritual crises, with their attendant backsliding, befall every observant Jew; they are certainly not unique to the *ba'al teshuvah*, but he is especially sensitive to them, and their effects are likely to be much greater on him than on one who has lived a whole life in a religious framework. Why this special sensitivity? First, because the *ba'al teshuvah*, more than others, is involved in an ongoing process of change that makes his life situation inherently unstable and vulnerable to shock. Second, the process itself entails a heightened degree of self-awareness and self-criticism. Disturbances that a life-long observant Jew takes in stride assume major proportions for the *ba'al teshuvah*.

A person raised in the Jewish way of life is helped through such crisis points by long-established habits of observance. Be it a problem of routine, weariness, or even despair, that person tends to fall back on traditional ways. For the *ba'al teshuvah*, on the other hand, Jewish ways are not second nature but the result of protracted struggle. It is easier for him, in moments of vacillation, to fall back on his earlier, nonreligious ways. Another difference results from experience. The life-long observant Jew has confronted challenges to his way of life before and learned how to deal with them; the *ba'al teshuvah* has not. Thus he may anguish for months over a relatively minor setback before regaining his balance, if indeed he does so at all.

In this context, the *ba'al teshuvah* often suffers from a certain idealization of the "perfect Jew," based either on living models glimpsed from a distance or archetypes out of the past. Such a person is imagined to be completely at one with himself and his chosen path, knowing no failure in its pursuit. Comparing himself to this ideal figure, the stumbling *ba'al teshuvah* experiences radical self-doubt.

The truth is that such ideal types, people who know no backsliding, have never existed except as figments of the imagination and of literary invention. No Jew, even the greatest leader, saint, or prophet, has ever been free of religious problems, failings, heartaches, and doubts. This is an established principle: everyone who takes the religious life seriously and who is thus ever striving onward experiences setbacks along the way. It is not merely that "there is no one so righteous that he does only good and never sins," but more than this: temptation, doubt, pain, and transgression are the inevitable lot of those who would ascend higher. To be sure, all seekers are not on the same level, and their failings are thus not equally grave. A great person who falls back may still be on a much higher plane than others. In both the material and the spiritual realms, "the righteous man may fall down seven times and yet arise." Though he falls again and again, he continues to grope his way upward. Indeed, this is the strength of the righteous: their ability to endure crisis, to bounce back, and to turn failure into a source of strength. "The [thoroughly] wicked man," on the other hand, "falls once and for all"; once down, he cannot get up. His way is blocked, and there is no way for him to renew his ascent.

Thrice daily, in the *Shmoneh-Esreh* prayer, we say, "Forgive us, for we have sinned." Though we fail, the way of return and the possibility of carrying on and succeeding are always open to us.

Each spiritual crisis has its own causes and remedies. It is important to remember in every case, however, that such crises are part of the process of religious life, not a negation of it. This process entails making one's way from stage to stage, laboring at every point to reshape one's inner life. Each upward movement entails a disruption of equilibrium—a jarring experience, to be sure, but a necessary part of the process. And the loftier and farther-reaching the aspiration, the greater the possibility of collision and breakage along the way.

Such crises are usually precipitated by marginal factors. Rarely in real life (as opposed to literature) is one suddenly afflicted with a powerful temptation from out of the blue. More commonly there is a gradual, barely perceptible slippage into a situation in which one's faith, principles, and mode of thought are no longer operational, so that sooner or later transgression is inevitable.

There are no tricks for ensuring that one will not trip and fall, no matter how righteous one has been or for how long. The Talmudic sages deal with this problem, but after lengthy analysis and numerous examples they fall back on the generalization that no one is safe from temptation; consequently, no one is in a position to despise backsliders. Over the years one learns one's own weaknesses and how to overcome or at least circumvent them. One learns to create for oneself those inward and outward circumstances most conducive to continued progress, without fear of experimentation or others' contempt. One who is unfamiliar with such problems or, *even more so*, one who has never built up for himself a way of life that can serve as a bulwark against them is much more likely to stumble.

When is this most likely to happen? There is no general rule. Indeed, there are pitfalls in every situation. At times, everything seems to be going well, one feels confident that one has achieved the "way of faith" and is progressing ever higher. Suddenly one falls into utter degradation and shame. This feeling of shame does not spring from piety alone, and the end result is revulsion, weariness, and despair. This is what the righteous of various generations meant when they said that even the worst transgression is not as bad as the dejection it leads to. There is no limit to the depths to which the human spirit can sink.

The greatest danger is that the sinner may sink to a level from which he can no longer raise himself. Sometimes an accidental and quite trivial occurrence can cause a person to abandon an entire hallowed way of life. Then, out of oversensitivity about his fallen state, he may continue for years to live in sin. The seriousness of individual lapses should not be minimized, but neither should even the worst of them be allowed to lead to despair and total abdication. "The righteous man may fall down seven times and yet arise" describes the real-life experience of one who stumbles from time to time along the way, yet, no matter how painful the fall, always picks himself up, mends what can be mended, and moves on. One who persuades himself that his very vulnerability to failure is a sign that he was never serious or sincere to begin with has rationalized a fatal descent.

All of a person's actions reveal different facets of his particular truth, but it would be false to speak of "the truth" as if it were something simple that could be uncovered once and for all. Every person's truth is complex and his nature a composite of conflicting tendencies. It is not just a matter of "the good impulse" and "the evil impulse." Furthermore, in the spiritual world, as in the physical world, there is no action without a reaction. A person who confronts the necessity of making a change in his life or of pressing on with renewed determination must also reckon with internal resistance, partly conscious and immediate, partly unconscious and revealed only with the passage of time. He cannot simply "turn over a new leaf" and start afresh; even after he sets out on his new path he will be hounded by those parts of him that remain unreconciled to his decision. The very struggle to ascend gives one the feeling of being at the bottom of the ladder; but this is only a trick of the senses and the imagination, for the ascent is, in fact, well underway.

Crises other than lapses or falls also afflict the *ba'al teshuvah*. The spiritual thicket in which he is likely to get entangled has many byways, and his entanglement is not necessarily the result of any single event. Aside from crises of faith (which I will discuss in the next chapter), there are also *periods* of distress, related to fluctuations in mood. Sometimes the problem begins with a sense that one is stuck in one place and not "progressing," that one does not have the strength or will power to move on, but that, nonetheless, one must somehow advance.

Such situations are not unique to *ba'alei teshuvah*. Stagnation occurs even more often with people raised in the religious tradition. But it is only to people of special religious sensitivity, like *ba'alei teshuvah*, that remaining spiritually static presents a problem. The origins of the problem are, as a rule, not particularly deep, not the result of any great internal or external resistance or of a loss of interest. Hence the solution may lie in simply making an effort to take a single additional positive step: doing another *mitzvah* or doing the same one better. Here it is important, especially for *ba'alei teshuvah*, to recall that there are many ways of taking significant steps forward, that action and involvement are not necessarily dependent on enthusiasm or even whole-hearted assent. Often, "we shall do" must precede "we shall hear"; though "not yet ready," one must sometimes undertake to do the thing nevertheless. In this, as in many spheres of the creative life, practice must often come before deliberation, mechanical action before inner readiness, work before inspiration. Then, some measure of inner engagement is bound to follow. One must make the initial decision to take a "leap" beyond the accustomed bounds of one's existence. Assuming a new "yoke," then, usually has a broadly refreshing effect, challenging every area of life that has become stale.

Another problem likely to be encountered, not only at the beginning but at every stage along the way, is that of spiritual fatigue, the waning of interest, and the loss of enthusiasm for the enterprise as a whole or some part of it. At times it may be just ordinary weariness due to excess tension and hard work.

When one assumes heavy new obligations, when one plunges into a new world of technical and spiritual demands, one is prone to overdo things in a way that leads to "overload," thence to fatigue and enervation. It is like what happens to a devotee of art who spends hours walking around a museum until he reaches a point of surfeit, of diminishing returns, beyond which new sights do nothing but tire him out. In such cases, the best remedy is to take a rest, to suspend the overly strenuous effort, and to allow the soul some breathing space to recover its powers of absorption. In the case of the *ba'al teshuvah*, it requires a spiritual respite, a temporary disengagement from the intensity of his Jewish quest in favor of more neutral, less demanding pursuits. Remember, just as an occasional break makes for greater efficiency at work, so too can the spiritual pursuit be renewed and revived by pausing from time to time to recoup, as long as one keeps clearly in mind that one *is* merely resting from one's efforts and not abandoning anything, that one is "descending in order to ascend." Without such respite, one runs the risk that one's efforts will gradually cease to provide any satisfaction or inner fulfillment, so that either one falls into a pattern of empty "stability" and meaningless routine or one abandons the enterprise altogether.

The weariness or disaffection may not be from Judaism in its totality but from some particular aspect of it, some area of practice or study. In such cases it should be recalled that, while the Torah in its entirety belongs to every Jew, each of us also has a particular "portion in the Torah," a part for which we have a special affinity, and other parts with which we resonate less. As the Sages said, "Let a man always study what, and with whom, his heart desires." Though one must strive ultimately toward completeness, it is permissible, particularly when first setting out, to concentrate one's efforts on those areas to which one's heart most readily responds, at the expense of other things. Then, too, negative feelings toward some aspect of Jewish religiosity may have a superficial cause: a poor teacher, an incorrect method of study, or inappropriate timing. Or the cause may be temporary, so that after the passage of time what seemed wearisome, unappealing, or even repugnant may become more appealing. Even so, it is best to avoid conflict and turn one's attention to that which has greater natural appeal.

As I have said, everyone, no matter how far along in spiritual development, is likely at times to experience weariness, an "inability to carry on," and meaninglessness. Even one who has followed the path of Torah and *mitzvot* wholeheartedly all his life can be overtaken by such fatigue and indifference. The root of the problem probably lies in a prior experience, somewhere along the way, of backsliding and "falling." Even the most pious and scholarly are not immune. The only cure for fatigue of this kind is spiritual renewal, and this, in turn, must come from outside. "A prisoner cannot effect his own release."

Herein lies the importance of comrades and close friends, with whom one can share one's concerns and from whom one can gain encouragement in times of crisis. Dark feelings often result from a sense that one has exhausted his own inner resources and cannot break out of the closed circle of his life. Talking the matter out, even indirectly, and examining it in the broader perspective of the fundamental sources of illumination can restore the soul to life. Even one not so afflicted is well advised to seek out renewal in contact with others, whenever the opportunity presents itself. To be sure, there is a danger here too of overdoing social contact, and rousing discussions do not always yield results. But it is important to make the effort and look for such reinforcement. If one has a rabbi or teacher who can serve one as a source of enlightenment, one should meet with him regularly. Lacking such a mentor, one should turn to friends, or even strangers, to help him sustain his inner life.

In the final analysis, the secret of fellowship is to be found in this verse: "For should they fall, one can raise the other; but woe betide him who is alone and falls with no companion to raise him!" (Ecclesiastes 4:10). Just as ups and downs are a part of life in general, so crises and misgivings are part of the life of faith. Weakness does not afflict everyone at the same time, so that when one is afflicted there are others around to help him up. "Two are better off than one, in that they have greater reward for their labor." (Ecclesiastes 9:9).

══ 7 ══

Problems of Faith

Even one who has moved beyond his first grave doubts and hesitations and made his way deep into the world of Judaism remains subject to periods of uncertainty. The various questions that first obstructed his path sometimes return later on, in different forms, to haunt him. In addition, greater knowledge and familiarity can give rise to new questions. One may have had no difficulty accepting basic principles, but when they are spelled out in all their ramifications, heart and mind may at some point begin to resist. The problems may be practical, social, or familial in nature, but often they are problems of faith. The way they present themselves to an individual depends on his personality. Some encounter one problem at a time, others a barrage of them all at once.

Over and above all the specific questions, at such times of doubt the *ba'al teshuvah* may be plagued by the particularly deep and fundamental question of whether his very uncertainty represents an irreparable flaw, bound to undermine the entire structure of commitment. In fact, it does not. The notion that a committed Jew never asks any questions or has any doubts is completely unrealistic. Virtually all religious people, even those most celebrated for their piety, must grapple with uncertainty from time to time throughout their lives. Thus it is not the experience of doubt but its character and depth that differentiate one person from another. Great people and those on whom Divine revelation is bestowed ask questions of a higher order and out of more exalted reasoning than the rest of us, each seeking to plumb his own ways and the ways of the Holy One, blessed be He, according to his intellectual and spiritual level. It is a function, on the one hand, of the complexity of human nature and, on the other, of the contradictory character of reality itself. In addition, doubt is *part* of the process of human spiritual growth. Faith is not a package one receives all neatly wrapped and sealed and keeps that way, intact, forever. Nor is it, as people imagine, a single, final, irrevocable step, like the amputation of a limb.

Like the Jewish way as a whole, faith is a long, unending process of growth and change. Such a growth process entails accompanying pains, new additions that must be consolidated at each stage, and gaps that must be carefully filled in. As long as the process continues, special care must be taken at certain points, space for recuperation allowed at others. Faith is one of the attributes of human character; its scope and power are a function of both inheritance and cultivation. With rare exceptions, people who are musically gifted—to use an analogy—do not achieve full expression of their gifts unaided or all at once, but require nurture and training. The same is true of faith: a single "revelation" that solves everything is difficult to come by, and even one who has a deep religious experience must then expand on it and implant it firmly in his soul if it is not to remain merely an isolated incident.

Some people live with doubt more easily, while others experience it as a source of pain and anguish. For some, both physical and spiritual growth, are gradual, with simple, easy transitions from one stage to the next, while others reach every new stage in great leaps, requiring conscious, laborious confrontation with the problems entailed. In general, the question is part of the answer, and doubt is inherent in the process of faith. The danger lies not in the questioning itself but in the confusion that so often paralyzes the questioner, renders him helpless, and prevents him from moving on.

Problems of faith take many forms, but there are two main types: doubt and questioning. Questioning is not a simple matter, for its true causes are often hidden. Sometimes, a vague sense of discomfort, dissatisfaction, insecurity, or hesitation is the disguised end result, on an emotional level, of an accumulation of unanswered questions. It is also true, however, that some of the most troublesome questions can be merely a displacement onto the cognitive level of problems of quite a different character. As our Sages point out, a skeptical query is often the expression of a temptation or weakness unrelated to the ostensible object of concern, and as soon as the questioner finds the satisfaction he is really seeking, his questions, which seemed so rational and objective, appear to melt away of their own accord. Knowing a question's complex antecedents can make answering it easier. The answer then comes, not directly, but by way of various layers of the soul.

Doubt, on the other hand, usually arises from feelings of insecurity: "maybe it isn't true," "maybe it isn't important," "maybe there's no point to it." Such feelings are sometimes rationalized, but usually they appear out of nowhere, then disappear again, either immediately or after some nagging delay. Because these feelings are essentially irrational, no arguing with them avails, no "claims and counterclaims," as the sages of *Musar* put it. They should be treated like whimsical thoughts, neither indulged nor combated at length, for dwelling on them can lead only to confusion. Like a passing bad mood, they should not be taken too seriously; rather, one should try simply to bear the unpleasantness while it lasts and get on to other things as quickly as possible. For it often happens that too long a delay at any one stage along one's path gives rise to vague spiritual longings, which replace rather than lead to action. The result is emotional frustration and intellectual uneasiness. At such times, one risks giving way to a paralyzing bitterness and melancholy. Instead, one should try to keep moving, to strengthen oneself by increased study and observance, and, not least, to seek out companions who will stir the soul.

Such crises are opportunities not just to "bolster one's faith," but for reinforcement and inspiration on the highest level. The more painful the doubts, the clearer the need to ascend higher. Such pain should itself be seen as a normal side-effect of the process of growth. Its remedy is to rise to a higher level. The same longing for transcendence can be expressed both positively, as what it is, or negatively, as pain and doubt. Similarly, doubt can be merely the outward guise of feelings of inadequacy, resulting from conflicting attachments of body, soul, and conscious mind. When the underlying cause is uncovered, the outward symptoms change. This does not mean that insight alone is sufficient to solve all one's problems and temptations. But at least insight allows us to grapple with the underlying causes and not merely with symptoms.

Unlike doubt, which is largely emotional and devoid of any content except the impulse to self-destruction, *questions* of faith are basically conscious and rational, whatever their source in the depths of the soul. Some questions result from misunderstanding or ignorance. But the *ba'al teshuvah* may be beset by genuinely fundamental questions, which give rise to much struggle and attempted evasion. Many such questions are not only difficult and painful but inherently unanswerable—a problem as old as Moses, Job, and Jeremiah. It is appropriate to ask, indeed to give vent to them. Yet the answers may well be beyond human understanding. If we could know them, we would no longer be human: "If I knew Him, I would *be* Him." Since, in the very nature of reality, an unbridgeable gap exists between the infiniteness of the Divine and the finiteness of human beings, there can be no real or complete response to certain human questions. The only appropriate way of dealing with them is to study religion and its principles more deeply, in order to gain greater understanding of how those questions arise and why they cannot be answered.

Another kind of questioning grows out of a confrontation between differing world-views. Living in an alien non-Jewish philosophical, psychological, and social milieu—as all Jews do, even the most pious—it is inevitable that we absorb its basic assumptions and that, as a result, certain of our Jewish assumptions are called into question. (How can the Torah speak in such a way? How can such a seemingly unreasonable act be commanded?) Yet, upon closer examination the questioner often realizes that his problem is itself simply a function of a different outlook on life, one which he has chosen to replace, and that it is not inherently insoluble. The question may be nothing more than a reflex of a consciously discarded but still somehow deeply ingrained Marxist, psychoanalytic, or other theory, the phantom of a dead idea returned to haunt the living.

Questions grounded in one system of thought cannot be answered by another one. For example, one who does not believe in miracles, prophecy, or Divine providence cannot expect satisfactory answers to questions about matters of Torah, where such beliefs are taken for granted and fundamental. Here, too, careful scrutiny of the underlying assumptions behind the questions themselves may be more productive and may yield more satisfactory answers than apologetics.

All of this is not to deny the validity of questioning itself. Is the Passover Seder, that great and cherished observance, not based on a series of questions asked by all?

As to answers, they may be more or less convincing, depending on their cogency, the readiness of the questioner to be satisfied, and the persuasiveness of the answerer. The *ba'al teshuvah* may ask his question to someone who does not know how to answer, yet refuses to admit it and, instead, dismisses the question as though it were inconsequential. Then, too, even the deepest and truest answer may not be readily accepted, for questions do not arise in a vacuum. They emerge from certain predispositions, and it is sometimes necessary to change those predispositions, to prepare the ground, before an answer can truly be absorbed. A person hears particular teachings, and it may be only much later that he comes to grasp their meaning and accept them as answers to his questions. This is what the Torah means when it says, "The Lord has not given you a heart to know . . . until this day." Similarly, the Sages taught that one cannot fully grasp one's master's meaning until the age of forty. Thus teachers need not insist that their answers be accepted without reservation. It is better to try to clarify the questions, their underlying premises, and their interrelationships. Such clarification tends not only to reduce the number of questions, but also to lead more readily to genuine solutions. Quite often, the difficulty of answering a particular question (and the even greater difficulty in gaining acceptance for the answer) arises from the fact that it was not a very "smart" question to begin with. It is far harder to answer a foolish, confused, or poorly formulated question than one that is intelligent and well put. A question that is badly phrased often conceals the questioner's real concern. Then, no matter how well the question is answered, he remains frustrated.

There is much to be learned here from talmudic methodology. The study of the Oral Torah is largely a matter of posing questions, then answering them. While many are answered immediately, others remain "unresolved," "in need of further study," or "in need of much more study." The problem is that one cannot remain stuck forever on a complex issue; one must move on, setting that issue aside until later, when, as often happens, it may appear in a different light, turn out to be soluble in a different formulation, or cease to be an issue. This intellectual method of attacking difficult problems—at times by direct investigation, at other times in a roundabout fashion or by reformulation—is the very one by which progress is made in every branch of science. So it is in Judaism. If people have questions, they deserve to be taken seriously and, if possible, to be answered; but the search for the perfect answer must not be carried to a debilitating extreme. Avoiding that extreme calls for inner clarity, forward momentum, and spiritual maturity.

8

Seriousness and Restraint

The *ba'al teshuvah*, being what he is, tends to take his religious life quite seriously. Indeed, his seriousness is both the cause and the result of his *teshuvah*. Most people know about spiritual quests and the search for identity, but find such pursuits irrelevant to their own concerns. They do not question accepted values or consider radical changes in their way of life. The path that the *ba'al teshuvah* has taken is a reflection of the significance he attaches to such issues. Even one who does not begin out of the deepest motivations naturally starts to take Jewish matters more seriously once his religious odyssey is underway. What people raised in a religious environment take for granted as routine practice is often seen by the *ba'al teshuvah* as something enormously significant and compelling in all its details, be it a single *mitzvah* or the entire yoke of the *mitzvot*.

The *ba'al teshuvah* also undergoes a change in his estimation of himself. A person who imagines himself as complete and all-knowing suddenly discovers how little he knows and how much guidance he needs in the simplest things. Having to reorient himself in the most fundamental way, to relearn, as it were, his ABC's, and to reconstruct all his relationships, he is like a newborn babe. It is not uncommon in such situations to feel contempt for oneself and one's past, including one's own achievements and other erstwhile sources of pleasure, pride, and self-confidence. One learns, sometimes for the first time, the feeling of humility, for in his own eyes he is small, ignorant, and empty. By comparison with others farther along the Jewish path, he sometimes despairs of ever reaching a higher plane.

The result of all these feelings is a great fervor and seriousness of purpose, particularly in relation to the fine points of observance. As a "new man," in the process of being formed, the *ba'al teshuvah* eagerly absorbs all the guidance he can get, deferring to his teachers and rabbis, those he considers his spiritual superiors.

While such qualities are most evident in the *ba'al teshuvah*, they are desirable in everyone; the literature of religious guidance, including *Musar*, repeatedly emphasizes caution, strictness, respect, humility, and submission. Yet however important and desirable these things are, they can also be hazardous to one's spiritual well-being and development, particularly in the case of the *ba'al teshuvah*. In a sense, the abandonment of one equilibrium for another is the essence of *teshuvah*, but during the intervening period of instability there is a tendency to extremism and a vulnerability to things that would not bother someone more experienced in the religious life.

The terrible seriousness concerning all aspects of Judaism felt by many *ba'alei teshuvah* can lead them to a morbid melancholy. When everything about one's past seems questionable, if not utterly useless, the result can be demoralization, the loss of all ability to function, and a general crisis of the personality. Instead of *teshuvah* stimulating personal progress, it becomes a source of constraint, preventing a person from leading any kind of life whatsoever. A sort of spiritual death ensues, not only a withering of interest in trivial matters (which is appropriate), but a loss of interest in everything.

Short of complete apathy, to which people of different temperaments are prone to different degrees, extremism also has other pitfalls which, though they may be less morbid, are even more dangerous. One can lose his sense of proportion, his ability to distinguish between things of greater and lesser importance. The *ba'al teshuvah* may not only take a disproportionate interest in relatively minor matters; he can also lose sight of things of real importance and neglect his relationship to them. He may, for example, become concerned with the details of dress—such as the variations adopted by particular groups and peculiar to certain times and places—far beyond their actual significance. He may change his garb and manner of speaking to fit in with the group he has joined, and sometimes the very difficulty of doing this distorts his sense of proportion. Changing the color or style of his hat may make integration easier for him, but, being purely imitative, it can leave him as alien as before, except that now he is bereft of his sense of what is truly worth striving for. So it is with innumerable other details of law and custom which, while normally simple to fulfill, can become so absorbing that they exhaust one's strength to move on to the next stage. Indeed, this inability to distinguish the wheat from the chaff—sin from nonconformity, commandment from custom—can lead ultimately to an abandonment of the entire enterprise, for the accumulated mass of self-imposed detail can come to seem a meaningless burden. Yet, all along, choice was possible and permissible.

A similar phenomenon is frequently observed in the area of faith as well as of practice. One can go from believing nothing to believing everything, from utter skepticism to utter credulity and a desperate effort to convince oneself of a thousand and one notions that may be not only spurious but actually even forbidden. Acceptance of the Torah and the *mitzvot* turns into a kind of magical rite, belief in the Sages becomes blind reverence for other people who are not really worthy of such uncritical acceptance, and faith becomes hopeless fatalism.

Judaism emphasizes the connection (which is not only an etymological one) between *emunah* (faith) and *emet* (truth). A Jew is obligated not only to learn the law, but also to engage in the world of discussion of the Talmud and its commentaries, where critical thinking plays a crucial role. Unlike Christianity or the various cults, Judaism does not fear questions nor run away from them. It is not even afraid to leave questions open indefinitely. Indeed, Judaism's great strength is that it encourages questioning and does not demand blind acceptance of dogma.

Indiscriminate dogmatism, like zeal for the minor details of observance, carries a danger of the eventual collapse of the entire structure. One who tries to ingest too quickly a whole world of ideas, including the best and the worst among them, is likely to discover that he can as quickly vomit it out, again without discriminating between wise and foolish, important and trivial. But the real problem with mindless conformity in both behavior and thought is that it is inherently invalid. Faith without the power to question obviates the true study of Torah; observance without meaning detracts from the observance that is essential. The Sages say that Scripture teaches us the way of humility and faith. "I am ignorant and know not; like cattle have I been with Thee" does not mean that we should always be "ignorant" or "like cattle," but rather that the acceptance of beliefs is appropriate when it is "with Thee," not an outgrowth of one's relation to other people.

Another problem stemming from ignorance or lack of discrimination is the loss of belief in oneself. Not only *Musar* and the literature of religious guidance, but also *halakhah* and everyday custom, address themselves to different levels and types of human ability. They do not expect everyone to measure up to the same demands, or to do so all his life. All of us have our virtues and defects; some among us are lofty souls and are worthy of emulation. One must not confuse ought and is: mountain peaks may be a prominent feature of the landscape, but the low-lying plain between them is also important.

Inability to recognize this can lead the *ba'al teshuvah* (and others as well) to unrealistic expectations of himself, and thus inevitably to a sense of failure. The latter develops particularly in everyday settings like the workplace and the home, where gray routine is the rule, and compromise is required. Only the rare individual is capable of living day by day with a constant sense of sanctity. In the home, spouse, children, and daily chores impose a need for considerable flexibility. At work, one must relate to various personalities and their expectations. Whoever fails to prepare himself spiritually for these demands will experience bitter disappointments, misunderstandings, and quarrels. Worse, he is likely to see his values steadily eroded. The problem is often provoked by unnecessary, unrealistic demands. The normal rhythm of life, with its ups and downs, superficialities and exaltations, gives way to a futile obsession that can only lead to bitterness, suffering, and, ultimately, the destruction of many valuable things that might have survived and flourished had it not been for this pressure.

No perfect solution exists for any of these problems. If one is fortunate enough to find a teacher who can instruct him, not only *in* Jewish ways but in how to relate Jewish ways to each other and to the whole of life, he will be spared many difficulties. This task—negotiating one's way among competing claims and weighing their relative merits while actually living according to a certain pattern—is the hardest of all.

Lacking a teacher's assistance, it may be helpful, first, to make a point of investigating the relative importance of each observance, what is more essential and what less so, and not rest content with knowing merely what is required. To be sure, "light" *mitzvot* are as important as "heavy" ones, and sometimes custom carries greater authority in practice than *halakhah*. Nonetheless, it is important to be able to distinguish between wheat and chaff, so that one can establish a scale of priorities and know where to take a stand. When a person is clear about his goal and what is essential to strive for, he can usually shape the changing reality around him to his ends. But woe to him whose boat is overloaded and who casts off human passengers in order to save a cargo of rags.

Second, it is helpful to remember that it is both permissible and advisable to ask questions, even though not every question can be given an immediate, satisfactory answer. It may at times be legitimate, as it is with children, to put a questioner off until another time or another stage in his development. And he should pose his questions, as does the Wise Son in the Haggadah, in the spirit of really wanting to know. But there is nothing wrong with asking, as the long Jewish tradition of doing so attests; indeed, asking questions is an important part of the process of *teshuvah* in all its aspects.

Third, one must learn to smile. It is not advisable to do everything grimly and fearfully. Some things can be taken more lightly, and in many contexts cheerfulness is permissible. It is not only a matter of avoiding sadness, which the Sages considered the worst of sins, but of keeping a sense of proportion, saving one's seriousness and grim determination for situations where they are needed. Judaism presents a particularly difficult spiritual challenge, for it asks us to live a life of holiness, not in monastic seclusion, but out in the world. It is a challenge that calls for balance and a sense of humor.

═══ 9 ═══

The Relation to the Past

Part of the *ba'al teshuvah's* struggle is to blot out his previous life. *Teshuvah*, the turning that gives new meaning to everything in life, also casts a new and frequently harsh light on what has gone before. Even one whose past is not particularly stained by evil-doing is likely to see its residue—memories, dreams, relationships, actions—as a confusing distraction from the more important tasks at hand. All the more is this the case when past events provoke feelings of guilt and remorse. The problem is compounded by the many temptations and desires the *ba'al teshuvah* continues to feel despite his changed world-view. He is afraid, and rightly so, to return to familiar haunts, to resume earlier activities, to renew old ties, lest they prove irresistibly seductive, conflict-provoking, or embarrassing.

The leap the *ba'al teshuvah* makes at a certain point along his spiritual path includes the breaking of ties. Living simultaneously in opposed spiritual and social worlds is very difficult, and he often erects wide barriers in an effort to separate them. A parallel process takes place internally, on the plane of the spirit. Penitence leads to atonement and forgiveness; the essence of forgiveness is the *wiping away* of sin, a kind of rebirth of the sinner. Not only is it forbidden to remind the penitent of his sins, but atonement is itself a renewal, in which past trangressions are made null and void and virtually cease to exist. This principle is expressed in the dictum of the Sages, "The first days shall fall away." The earlier time no longer exists and is not even to be counted in the new reckoning.

But *teshuvah* is neither unambiguous nor unidirectional; it is multifaceted, while the *ba'al teshuvah* himself is a complex creature. It is not possible in life to expunge, once and for all, all trace of past events. In reality, *teshuvah* is a protracted, almost endless process. Remorse and penitence are required at every stage of elevation toward the Divine, with a level of repentance appropriate to, and sufficient for, each level of progress. The higher one goes, the fuller and more perfect the penitence required, until eventually it is not transgression for which atonement is sought but the lack of perfection in one's performance of *mitzvot*.

Teshuvah has two essential phases: a leap of disengagement from the past, and a lengthier, more arduous process of rectification. The first phase is one of destruction, the second of reconstruction. A person's sins never pass from this world entirely, nor are they simply forgotten; rather, they take on a different meaning. As the Sages put it, a person's deliberate sins are transformed into unwitting transgressions and, at a later stage, into virtues. This transformation is not automatic, but a process in which the *ba'al teshuvah* plays an active, conscious role.

In practice, there is no set pace at which the progression from stage to stage takes place. It depends on one's character and ability and on the quality of one's *teshuvah*. How long it will take from the time one makes the break with the past until one is ready—and feels the need—to rebuild on its ruins depends on how quickly one can achieve a sense of security in his new identity and how readily one can incorporate the Jewish way of life into his spiritual persona. Sometimes this transition is long drawn out, like slow recuperation from a life-threatening illness or recovery from a difficult and painful operation. But it must eventually come to an end. One cannot, indeed must not, spend one's whole life hiding, physically or spiritually, from one's surroundings, much less from oneself. Those who do, reveal weakness and impotence; but worse, they fail to *follow through* with the process of *teshuvah* that they originally undertook. The essence of *teshuvah* is not only in a person's return to his true place, but also in the restoration of his misdeeds, the spoiled parts of his life, to their true place.

This "*teshuvah* of reconstruction" is not just a matter of lofty spiritual reckoning; it is a psychological necessity. Just as there is no forgetfulness on high, so do both the good and the bad a person has done linger on within him. For better or worse, one cannot be rid of oneself. *Teshuvah* is a change, sometimes a complete reversal, of direction, but not the creation of a new being. In the final analysis, one's fundamental qualities, talents, and stores of knowledge go with him wherever he goes. One can, of course, try to ignore them and pretend they never existed, but the result is a superficial, merely behavioral change, a kind of play-acting behind a mask. Part of one will always be suppressed, constrained, and unfulfilled. It is not salutary to conceal and ignore an affliction; it must be healed.

We generally hold to the view that there is no such thing as absolute wickedness. Every blemish and distortion of character or behavior has its positive side. Our Sages long ago pointed out that things that at first glance appear evil can be directed toward worthy ends if one assesses them properly and recognizes their hidden potential. Even such negative qualities as arrogance and irascibility have their legitimate application. They are, in a sense, necessary ingredients in certain essential human activities, as necessary as talent, knowledge, or the very will to live.

The process of rectifying and recovering the past is not mechanical, to be performed in a certain set manner. It must take into account many factors, according to the circumstances of time, place, and opportunity. Even more significant is the nature of one's past misdeeds: how far they strayed from the true path and how they affected others. Failings of a more neutral nature, not laden with such great moral significance, may be more easily rectified—for example, defects of personality, knowledge , and skill, which in the process of *teshuvah* must be reckoned with as surely as past misdeeds.

One doing *teshuvah* need not leave his personality behind.

Great spiritual change does not necessitate a wholesale change of character. A person of intellectual ability and inclination, for example, may apply these qualities to the task of spiritual reorientation, finding an outlet for them in the study of Judaism, while more poetic individuals may pursue that path in Jewish study and activity. In matters great and small, there is room for differences of temperament, interest, and ability, and no need to force oneself to engage in things that are totally alien and unappealing. To be sure, Judaism does have definite general outlines, and one cannot simply pick and choose to suit his fancy. But within these limits there is a variety of possible emphases, a variety of realms in which different kinds of people can derive benefit and make their contributions. Judaism in its totality offers outlets for all the many factes of the human personality.

Everyone has a special gift in some particular field of endeavor, and in that field is called on to make a special contribution. The Sages say that in addition to keeping all the commandments, one should choose a single observance in which to be particularly scrupulous and diligent—"more careful," in the words of the Talmud. In this choice, one can be guided by the promptings of one's own heart and inclinations. As the masters of *Musar* said, one who has a talent for cutting precious stones should not be a lumberjack, for to do so would be to spurn a gift bestowed by the Creator.

The *ba'al teshuvah* must assess as accurately and objectively as possible his own interests and involvements. *Teshuvah* entails a change, sometimes quite radical, in one's order of priorities. Many things in which a person glories at one stage in life lose their appeal when confronted with the eternal values. Wealth, honor, peace of mind and personal satisfaction are transient things. Given the possibility of nearness to the Divine, of what worth can they be? On the other hand, we human beings do not live *only* in the presence of God. A large part of our lives is lived in this world, carrying out this-worldly tasks according to this-wordly scales of value. No doubt all matters of this world appear to shrink to insignificance when compared with the Infinite, but we cannot, indeed may not, judge our lives at every moment by this standard. We are also called upon to make judgments according to the relative, material standards of the human society we live in. The eternal and the sacred provide a gauge that helps us set priorities in our lives, but they do not negate all other measures of value.

Here, too, one must distinguish among the various stages of *teshuvah*. In the first stage, that of breaking with the past, one must give precedence to the great reckoning that exalts the eternal while diminishing the temporal. But once a stable new equilibrium is achieved, the latter must be reincorporated into one's life—chastened and put in proper perspective, but not rejected out of hand. Judaism's purpose is not to nullify or shun the world we live in, but to heal and perfect it. Monasticism—rejection of this world as mere vanity—cannot be our final aspiration. It is therefore necessary to reconsider and reevaluate material concerns in terms of their importance on a variety of levels. The businessman and the military man, the scholar and the simple worker fulfill valuable functions, however imperfect.

The proselyte, while regarded halakhically as a newborn child in many respects, brings much to his new life, both materially and spiritually, that he acquired previously, yet he is not required to cast everything aside and begin anew. How much more so the *ba'al teshuvah* must constructively engage his past, reassess it, and learn to see it in the proper light. One should not overestimate what has gone before, but neither should one underestimate it. Rather, seeing the past and its legacy clearly and accurately is an essential part of rectification and atonement.

In looking back, we focus on our blemishes and faults, not in order to wallow in guilt, but to use our flaws for leverage in the effort to progress. Not all deficiencies can be remedied, but some can and must be. As the holy Zohar tells us, *ba'alei teshuvah* are even more exalted than the saints, "for they are drawn to Him with greater force." Evil deeds, once recognized, become a constant goad and encouragement to reform. In this sense, they become virtues. Whoever has been remiss and sinned against society or other individuals must repay and restore what he can, be it money or otherwise. Whoever has been remiss, even slightly, and thereby caused others to sin must, through his own virtue, bring them back to the right path. Whoever has been unwittingly remiss must consciously make amends; and whatever damage has been caused by wrong-headedness must be rectified by rightheadedness. Life itself, including both past and present, mut be seen as a single whole. And it is the task of *ba'alei teshuvah*, at whatever age or stage, to live in such a way as to be able to say, "Happy is our old age, for it has atoned for our youth."

10

Heritage and Family

In Jewish tradition, the *ba'al teshuvah* is like a person without parents. Heritage—inherited mores, laws, practices, ways of living—does not exist for him in the usual way. Whatever the reasons for his *teshuvah*, it is a process that entails starting many things from scratch. Only rarely does it enable him to reestablish connections with his own past. The chain of transmission from generation to generation was, in the case of his family, broken at some point, and it is he who must pick it up again.

For all its detailed prescription, *halakhah* does not provide a monolithic set of rules for all aspects of religious life. In many of the areas it deals with—the liturgy and the dietary laws, for example—*halakhah* allows for legitimate variations in practice. In such cases it generally requires a person to follow the particular tradition he has inherited. Even more numerous are the questions of practice that do not fall within the purview of *halakhah* at all but are entirely matters of local or familial custom. The melodies used in prayer, the design of the *Kiddush* cup, the way the *tallit* bag is embroidered, the ingredients used in *cholent*—anyone who has visited a variety of synagogues or observant homes during a holiday can testify to the great differences

58

in these things from one place to the next. All are beautiful, all legitimate. How is one to choose? Questions of this sort may not be of great theological importance—if they were they would be governed by *halakhah*—but they do come up in daily life and must be resolved.

Custom is inherited. When families of different backgrounds are joined, there is inevitably a mingling of customs. The *ba'al teshuvah*, however, coming from a background devoid of religious practice, is at a loss. (Today, even in the Orthodox world, there are many people from such backgrounds.) The *ba'al teshuvah* may take one of two paths: either to join an existing community and adopt its halakhic traditions and customs, or to choose eclectically from a variety of traditions those practices that impress him or for which he feels a special affinity, synthesizing his own personal pattern from these diverse components.

Both of these alternatives raise halakhic questions, questions that, given the relative recency of the *teshuvah* phenomenon, have not yet been fully addressed or resolved. A problem on a different level also arises: one's personal sense of continuity or discontinuity. This problem equally affects the one who adopts an existing pattern of observance and the eclectic person.

Judaism is not just a matter of individual commitment. However personal one's involvement may be, Judaism always entails a linkup with past and future generations. Nor can this linkup be entirely abstract; it must at some point be mediated by an actual familial connection. The meaningfulness of such a connection, if it is not immediately apparent to the *ba'al teshuvah*, becomes so when he reaches the point of trying to pass the tradition on to the next generation. It is not enough merely to transmit information about what *halakhah* requires; a human context must be provided. A life lived only "by the book" is cold and dry. Customs derive their vitality from associations—with people, events, or experiences—and these must be acquired personally. Furthermore, when the question of continuity arises, it is hard to make a case for a seemingly arbitrary identification with a particular group.

The tie with the adoptive group, lacking deep roots, is necessarily a tenuous one. Nor does shaping one's personal or family life according to a disembodied tradition allow for *indivi-duation*. Paradoxically, individuation is far easier in traditional society; where tradition is taken for granted as the framework of everyday life, individual participation in that framework is less stereotyped. Monolithic societies are not the product of tradition but of totalitarianism; their growth is mechanical and artificial rather than organic.

For all these reasons, one taking up Jewish religious life must not forsake his own historic roots, but must actively seek them out. Grandparents, ever a source of family lore, may also be living examples to be emulated. If one's grandparents are no longer accessible, it may still be possible to trace one's Jewish roots back to earlier generations. Such a search amounts to an acceptance, not merely a reluctant acknowledgement, of the pluralism and diversity in Jewish tradition. Even in Ezekiel's messianic vision, there are separate gates to the Temple for each of the twelve tribes. The Sages explain these as being different gates for different people, "each of the Israelites remaining bound to the ancestral portion of his father's tribe" (Numbers 36:7). Here we see not an inability to unite but a recognition of human diversity. Similarly, the Sages describe Elijah's role at the time of the final redemption as that of restoring the Israelites, one by one, to their tribes and families. Israel is to be united, not as the result of a blurring of the differences among the tribes, but when each can relate to the others on the basis of confidence in, and open expression of, its own distinctiveness.

The search for roots, even in the simplest genealogical sense, is likely to be a meaningful experience on both the personal and religious levels. But it is important to pursue it even if the meaning is elusive. Lineage is not just a matter of empty self-congratulation. All lineage, and not just that of nobility, carries with it a certain responsibility. A great person discovered among one's ancestors is not just a cause for bragging but something that must be related to and learned from. The sense of kinship with such a figure can be a source of strength and encouragement to one suffering spiritual distress or self-doubt. It need not be a famous or distinguished figure; even a person— remembered or reconstructed—who was at one with himself and with the world can serve as an anchor point and source of commitment. Such connections represent, in a sense, a broadening of the commandment to "honor thy father and thy mother," a commandment described through the ages in terms of the obligation of the "branch" toward the "root" from which it sprang and that nourished it. Honor of parents and of earlier generations of forebears is connected, in turn, with *kibbud hamakom*, honoring the source of all human life. Strengthening one's ties with one's own past is part of renewing one's connectedness with the sources of Jewish life in general.

Beyond the memories and quasi-memories of one's forebears, there is also a practical significance in recovering their particular traditions. Though one may not be able to reconnect fully with the particular community they belonged to, one can at least adopt certain of their practices. Halakhically, this would not constitute following *minhag hamakom* or *minhag mishpahah* (local or family custom), but it could be highly meaningful. The very knowledge that a certain custom, style, or version comes down to one from one's own ancestors makes it compelling and alive in a way that can be very important for sustaining observance. Certain details, insignificant in themselves, can give one the feeling of following in his ancestors' footsteps, and this adds a dimension of warmth and intimacy to what might otherwise be a mechanical act. The very fact that one is giving new life to something with which one has an inner connection is meaningful.

From another less obvious point of view, an individual's relationship to a particular manner of observance is determined by his family's relationship to it. The tribes enter the sanctuary through the gates designated for them, though there are other ways of getting in. A given Jewish community's insistence on a particular way of doing things is not just a matter of obstinacy. It reflects a prolonged, only partly conscious process of natural selection over many generations in which certain ritual affinities form and are stengthened. There is an inner connection between a particular community or family and its customs. Thus the *ba'al teshuvah*, returning to the primary sources of his Jewish being, is bound to feel an especially deep resonance with those forms of expression associated with his own origins, and these forms are likely to serve him best in his quest for himself.

The search for familial roots and customs can be pursued

in a variety of ways. Sometimes one discovers a great many relatives one did not know he had and realizes, too, that his relationship to them can be more than casual. Such encounters can provide a person with new ways of seeing himself. One can also learn a great deal from books describing life in the localities where one's family lived.

Of course, one also must exercise caution. Carried away with the sense of identification, one can lose sight of the ineradicable distance between the generations caused by differences in time and place. The affinity one sometimes feels for certain forebears, or the warmth and "homyness" one experiences in certain company, do not necessarily signify complete identity with them. Appearances can be deceiving. One cannot always "return" to the past, however much one may wish to. Nonetheless, while one can live without roots, it is better to hold on to them. It is especially valuable for the ba'al teshuvah, who must sever so many of the connections in his life, to replace them with others. It is good for a Jew to know that, for all the loneliness his personal choice imposes on him, his life is nonetheless a continuation and an offshoot of a whole world that preceded him.

The process of finding one's roots, of establishing a bond with previous generations, gives rise to certain problems. The same person who makes contact with his past and connects up with his grandfather and the entire historic lineage of his ancestors may find that he is thereby cutting himself off from his immediate family—parents, brothers, sisters, and other contemporary relatives. Obviously, there is no fixed pattern to all of this; every individual has unique ways of relating to his family. In many instances, a repentant younger member of the family carried the whole family with him and enabled them to reunite in a more significant manner than before. In other cases, the parents or others in one's circle relate with sympathy and love to someone who has chosen the old-new way. It happens, too, that a person who boldly presumes to take what he feels to be a difficult and even rather strange path discovers that he is actually expressing the secret wishes of his parents. The parents themselves may be too absorbed in their own world or they may be unable to change their way of life because of emotional pressures and memories from their own childhood. Nevertheless, they may have a sympathetic and even encouraging attitude to the efforts of a child of theirs to crash through the barrier, even if the gap between them is not bridged.

In many other situations, however, parents and relatives feel they have lost all contact with the one who has become *ba'al teshuvah*, thus giving rise to many negative feelings, from sudden estrangement to unreasonable antagonism and even bitter enmity. These feelings may spring from a genuine conflict of ideas about religious and secular philosophies and approaches to life, or they may stem from hidden guilt feelings, repressed hatred, and the like, which burst forth in the conflict over religion. Frequently the negative feelings revolve around love and hurt over its apparent loss, when it seems (especially to devoted parents) that the child is transferring his love elsewhere. Such a reshuffling of intimate relationships is reminiscent of what sometimes happens when an undesirable marriage partner is chosen and the parents react by cutting themselves off, not only from the spouse but even from their own child.

The *ba'al teshuvah*, like someone who marries, may find himself in a state of conflict that is far from simple—the new connection may be more intense and passionate, but it is difficult to make a clear and final choice between the present and the previous loves. To be sure, the matter does not always depend on the *ba'al teshuvah*; it is not up to him alone to determine the nature of the new relationship between him and his family.

At the same time, everyone can at least try to do certain things—and it is important that the *ba'al teshuvah* do them, for his own sake, for the sake of his family, and no less so for the sake of his Jewishness. Often the *ba'al teshuvah* is so absorbed in his inner world and his new problems that he has no room in his soul to relate to other people. This sort of severance from other people is in every instance a self-contradiction; anyone who has no place in his world for other people has no place for God either. The first step for a person who makes such a transition is to try to understand and, as far as possible, to respect others. To understand others means, in this context, to try to see the point of view of his parents and family. Even if a person is convinced he is right and the others are mistaken, he should try to understand what they think and how they feel. Only in extreme cases, when every confrontation leads to a quarrel, is there cause to remove oneself.

In every case, it should be emphasized that the transition to a new spiritual world does not necessarily mean a thrusting away of everything that belongs to the other world. This emphasis is necessary precisely because sometimes when a person changes his lifestyle, others do not understand it or his new behavior toward them, and they view it as offensive or as an abandonment of the old relationship. When the *ba'al teshuvah* is conscious of these reactions to his actions, he should realize that he has to renounce preaching and try to explain himself, his reasons, and the new framework of his life. He must remember that the *mitzvot* to honor one's parents and to bring kin together are not dependent on the personal nature of the relationship but on the very connection itself. The Sages have explained that the *mitzvah* to honor one's father and mother is like the *mitzvah* of honoring the Divine, of showing respect for the Creator, for the root of life. Even if one thinks one's parents are not on the right path, one still has to honor them and come close to them. Anyone who tries to force his own way of life on others cannot expect them to accept him with love.

As the Sages have said, "Just as it is a *mitzvah* to say something that will be listened to, so it is a *mitzvah* to refrain from saying that which will not be listened to." It should also be kept in mind that the prohibition against quarreling is no less important than any other prohibition; therefore, wherever relationships become ruptured, it is preferable to effect a reconciliation. This does not mean that the *ba'al teshuvah* has to relinquish his own ideas if they are not to the liking of his family. He simply has to cling to existing connections and relationships in spite of all the differences.

11

Social Relations

Each of us is a distinct entity, as well as a part of the society he lives in. Our social circles are many and varied, from family and friends, to school and workplace, neighborhood and polity. In some cases the ties are close, emotional, and deliberate, while in others they are casual or involuntary. A Jew also has ties with the larger entity of the Jewish people: the synagogue where one prays, comrades in study, etc. Along with all these types of relationships go a variety of mutual influences.

Among the many changes that take place in the process of *teshuvah* are changes in the *ba'al teshuvah*'s relationship to the society around him. These changes may be so drastic as to require pulling up stakes and moving to an entirely different society, where a whole new network of relations must be established. Sometimes the process of *teshuvah* undergone by one individual dovetails with similar changes in the lives of those close to him, as when a husband and wife decide to set out on such a path together. Here, too, where the nuclear family remains intact, there are changes in relationships with wider social circles: the extended family, neighbors, colleagues, etc.

From both the practical and the subjective points of view,

a conflict arises here. On the one hand, there is the power of inertia, a tendency to hang on to old, established ties and relationships. In some cases this is unavoidable; no matter what changes one undergoes, he cannot break off completely with his family or other loved ones, nor can he always make sudden changes in his residence or place of work even if he wants to. On the other hand, the essence of *teshuvah* lies precisely in severing oneself from the past and reevaluating everything associated with it. There may be nothing inherently wrong with one's previous associations, which may have been based on factors of a "neutral" character, remote from sacred concerns; yet such associations may have been predicated also on purposes and ways at variance with those of Judaism. In addition, the process of *teshuvah* entails a certain turning inward that weakens all previous external ties, no matter what their character.

This conflict arises in an objective way, without regard to questions of right and wrong. It is impossible for one to insulate oneself completely from the influence of the surrounding society. The stronger and more emotional the bonds, the greater the influence. But seemingly cool, detached, mechanical relationships also inevitably exert their effects. And even when one finds oneself in hostile surroundings, when one deliberately tries to fend off the environment or when that environment, in turn, rejects him, one is still affected by its influence. Of course, the effects are not necessarily unidirectional. Just as society draws the hostile individual in, it may also have the countervailing effect of *strengthening* him in his opposed way of thinking and behaving and his ability to resist.

The problem of the *ba'al teshuvah*'s relation to society is especially complex in another way. Because he does not "inherit" a ready-made world of values and practices but must enter one that is strange to him and make it his own, he is especially sensitive to the role of social influences in his life and in need of social support. Halakhically speaking, one must have at least two social frameworks in order to function today as a Jew: the family, which is required for the fulfillment of a whole set of *mitzvot*, and the *minyan*, which is needed to fulfill the communal aspects of Judaism—the Jews as "the congregation of the Lord," represented by ten men who pray together. But this is not enough. One also needs a place to study, a social infrastructure in which to educate one's children, facilities for the observance of *kashrut*, a *mikvah*, etc. And on the spiritual plane, there is a need for the reinforcement and example a community provides.

Even one who has made his own way to Judaism, overcoming many internal impediments, experiences difficult phases. Sadness and anxiety are a part of the human condition. Likewise, the routine of life tends to dull the most poignant of experiences, turning religious observance (in this case) into empty, mechanical ritual. Here, a supportive social context can help stabilize the individual. One person's temporary setback is balanced out by the forward movement of others, so that individuals are carried along by the momentum of the collective and not allowed to fall by the wayside altogether. Each person has his weaknesses and strengths, things he can contribute to the community, and those for which he needs its help.

Even more than he needs the community's reinforcement, the *ba'al teshuvah* needs the example of the community in fashioning for himself a way of life. The entire edifice of the *mitzvot* is in reality no more than a framework, a skeleton on which a way of life can be formed through a variety of possibilities, with many subtle, yet meaningful, variations. Putting flesh and sinew on the skeleton is a matter of experience, that cannot be accomplished without living human models. This does not mean slavish imitation down to the last detail, which is virtually impossible in any case. The living example does provide more effective training than any theoretical instruction. This is what the Sages had in mind when they said, "Service [rendered to scholars] is greater than study." One who serves a true sage and spends time in his company derives guidance from every moment, not just from what his teacher explicitly says, but also from what he does.

For all these reasons, it is imperative that the *ba'al teshuvah* find a real Jewish social setting for himself as quickly as possible. Even when all his previous relationships still appear to be intact, he needs to find a new framework, a framework for his spiritual and corporeal life as a Jew. Choosing such a framework is not easy. To be sure, one is likely soon enough to come across a group that seems suitable, either because of geographical proximity or because one happens to know people who are

members, and this group—it could be a local congregation—
can prove quite adequate to one's needs over a long period of
time, perhaps indefinitely. But it should not necessarily be seen
as a permanent haven. Sometimes it is best to keep looking
until one finds a setting that suits one in every way.

A suitable community will not necessarily be one of great
or saintly persons, but it should be one that offers most of the
things for which a community is needed. Let us consider two
of these things, expressed in the saying, "Make for thyself a
master and acquire for thyself a comrade." The first part of this
maxim has been understood by the various commentators down
through the generations as meaning that each person must
commit himself to a particular person whom he thenceforth
sees as his mentor and guide. Such choices are often arbitrary.
It is in the very nature of things that one cannot *examine* a
prospective master for the breadth of his knowledge, much less
for the depth of his Jewish spirituality. Nonetheless, though the
choice be made haphazardly and as a result of incidental circumstances and connections, it is of great importance and
should be done as soon as possible. As long as the person is
someone worth learning from—a function, not only of his
knowledge but of his inner authenticity, his identification in
faith and deed with the principles he propounds—it matters
little whether or not he is the greatest scholar or saint of his
generation. A God-fearing master who runs up against a halakhic or practical problem he cannot solve can be counted
on to take it to those who can. Indeed, it is a firm rule that
any scholar worthy of the name is capable of saying "I don't
know." On the other hand, if one fails to "make for himself a
master" but goes from one person to another, soliciting opin-
ions and trying to draw his own conclusions, he has no real
teacher at all. Furthermore, it is important that when one does
adopt a master, he take his instruction with utmost seriousness,
be it lenient or stringent. Never should one ask a master's advice unless he is prepared to follow it, whatever it may be.

The choice of a master is not just a matter of finding an
address where halakhic advice of various kinds can be obtained. Even more important is the advice a master can give
about matters that are not strictly halakhic but fall between
the forbidden and the inappropriate, the permissible and the

praiseworthy. It is in these gray areas that one is most in danger of becoming a "rogue with the permission of the Torah," in the harsh phrase of the Sages; nothing, on the other hand, is more likely to drive a person away from Judaism than the attempt to live completely within what he has defined for himself as "*halakhah*." "Making for oneself a master" is thus finding a person who can help one solve problems and ease doubts and difficulties. This does not mean that one should unload all of one's problems on someone else or give up thinking or making painful decisions. No person may—indeed, can—simply give over his mind and heart to another, making himself into a dumb instrument of the other's will. Even those who take counsel with and accept the authority of the greatest sages of Israel still have problems, questions, and misgivings. It is the teacher's role, rather, to serve as an objective yardstick, utterly devoid of self-interest, close to his disciple, supportive of him, and seeking only to help him in his struggle to reach sound conclusions.

The same is true of "acquiring a comrade." In a meaningfully Jewish society, one is not only tied to the collective in a formal, mechanical, halakhic way; one also takes on a certain lifestyle in the broadest sense. Much of Jewish life is not defined halakhically at all, or only loosely so. For example, there may be a Jewish manner of dress and speech, a Jewish way of spending leisure time. Integration into Jewish society involves far more than attendance at public functions (worship, study, etc.); it also involves a kind of behavioral adaptation. And for this, as for more spiritual things, the support and companionship of peers is important. Such adaptation is significant, in turn, for how one will be perceived by others. How one dresses or conducts oneself is bound to evoke an immediate response from those around. Those who sense kinship with him will be drawn closer, those who sense distance will keep away; thus he will find himself in the company of those whose company he really wants. But not knowing just what to do in these subtle, gray areas can be a problem and a source of embarrassment and tension.

One may assume that a particular way of doing things is completely neutral and meaningless from a religious point of view; indeed, in the abstract one may be right. Yet things like dress, manner, and livelihood can lead to conflicts between what one believes is right to do and what one actually does. Problems of this kind can be even more difficult for the family than for the lone individual. It is in one's relationship with one's spouse and in the raising of children that the deep splits in the individual's life will be revealed. A contradiction or inconsistency may be manageable when other people are not involved, but as soon as they *are* involved it becomes a dangerous abyss they can easily stumble into. Thus, attachment to a proper social framework becomes essential for anyone taking a Jewish religious commitment seriously.

In relation to both mentor and friend, the personal element plays an important role. Affinities between people are a function of irrational, subjective factors as much as objective ones. One cannot will a sense of closeness to another person, however worthwhile it may seem. To be sure, one does have a certain amount of control over these matters, especially those who, like certain saints, are "masters of their own hearts" and can open them to the right people. But even here, some will inevitably be closer than others. As a general rule, one should not pick a companion purely on the basis of his virtues; one should also consider the interpersonal chemistry.

On a group level, too, an impromptu *minyan* of ten strangers differs greatly from one made up of people who come from the same background and who thus share spiritual roots and often respond to things the same way. A *minyan*, and even an entire community, can be just a collection of individuals; but a "family" is a single entity, the parts of which are like the limbs of a body. And because of the deep bond among family members, influence and inspiration flow more readily and more intensely. Consequently, whenever one comes to choosing a new social group, he should again ask himself not only whether it is worthy of his interest or whether he is in agreement with it on an intellectual plane, but also whether he feels a sense of kinship with its members.

It is also worth dwelling on the meaning of "making" a master and "acquiring" a comrade. These things cannot be left to chance, and even a prolonged search for the "right" person will not suffice. Rather, what is called for is conscious choice and the active cementing of a relationship. One can search for the "perfect" teacher or friend his whole life long to no avail.

Indeed, the *ba'al teshuvah*, with his ability to uproot himself socially and intellectually and to walk untrodden paths, is particularly prone to endless wandering. "Make for thyself a master" means make a decision and take a stand. There are well-known cases of people who were outstanding individuals in their own right, with much to contribute as teachers themselves, who, nonetheless, for the sake of their own development, accepted the authority of others they saw as being on a higher plane. Eventually one may move on to other masters, other social attachments; but it is important at any given point to make a firm commitment and stick with it for as long as it takes to build a stable spiritual edifice for oneself. Such commitments need not last forever, but neither should they be seen as mere dabbling or experimentation. Once a choice is made, it should be solidified, developed, and built upon. As the Sages said, "He who establishes for himself a place of prayer will be aided by the God of Abraham." The fixing of such a place, be it for prayer, for the study of Torah, or for fellowship, creates a vessel for the beneficence of Him who comes to the aid of seekers.

Finding a circle of close friends within a Jewish framework satisfies important needs on the part of the isolated *ba'al teshuvah*. But it leaves unresolved the question of what to do with one's past network of associations. In this regard, each individual is different. For some, it is better to make a clear, decisive break, abandoning one's previous circle completely for a while, so that he can eventually renew contact with it as a different person on a different footing. This procedure, for all its difficulties, is likely to be most helpful to the sensitive, hesitant type of person in recovering his social and spiritual equilibrium. The inner transition is difficult enough for such people without being complicated by struggles with a recalcitrant social environment. The change he is making in his life is not, after all, confined to abstract ideas, but reaches down to the minutiae of everyday life. Activities like joking, playing, and eating can no longer be pursued in the same way as they once were. Yet any attempt to change course and pull away in the midst of a relationship generates tensions. Such difficulties can also be avoided by making changes during the natural breaks afforded by vacations and trips, following which one can return to the same setting on a new basis. Of course, temperament or a variety of external factors may prevent some people from using such opportunities.

A third alternative is to determine what changes relevant to social activity one definitely wants to make, then simply to tell one's friends about them as clearly as possible. The position of such a person, midway on his journey, may seem somewhat ludicrous, for his friends can rightly point to a dual lack of consistency in his behavior: he insists on things that never mattered to him, and he is strict about some things but not others. However, it is best in this situation simply to make plain one's stance and not engage in elaborate attempts to justify or rationalize it. Such rationalizations are often unconvincing and only make one's position look even more ridiculous. More than this, they often entangle one in a web of lies, big and small, or unwelcome compromises. For example, a person who decides to refrain from traveling on *Shabbat* does both himself and his friends a favor, in the last analysis, by telling them about it. What is more, he may well find that his apprehensions about friction with them are unfounded, that his best friends turn out to be not only understanding but also helpful.

Another kind of social problem stems from the innocent enthusiasm the *ba'al teshuvah* often feels for his newly chosen path. This enthusiasm can take the form of relentless preaching and badgering, in which he tries to persuade his family and friends to "taste of the fruit of the Tree of Life." Having been fortunate enough to find his way, he wants to share his good fortune with those close to him, and, being a product of their world, he can often be quite persuasive. But he must be careful to avoid overdoing it, thus becoming obnoxious and making a nuisance of himself. Over and above purely human considerations, there is a matter here of *kiddush hashem* and *hillul hashem*—of sacred witness. The preachy, self-righteous *ba'al teshuvah* becomes intolerable, so that instead of drawing others nearer to religion, he actually drives them further away. Here, as elsewhere, "walk humbly" is an admirable rule, and personal example speaks louder than any sermon. If he truly wants to have a positive effect on others, the *ba'al teshuvah* should strive to be what the Sages called "beloved on high and cherished below," fulfilling and overfulfilling his obligations to others and letting them draw their own conclusions.

═══ 12 ═══

Jews and Non-Jews

For Jews, the question of relations with the non-Jewish world arises in many areas of everyday life. In the Diaspora, where the question is more likely to arise in the interpersonal sphere, it is more pressing and concrete. But the issue is also a real one in Israel. This is not a matter of concern only for the *ba'al teshuvah*, of course. But a person who is trying to disengage himself from non-Jewish things is likely to find the issue more immediate.

The relationship between the Jewish people and the nations of the world is a complex, multifaceted, ever-changing one, involving questions of principle and a significant sediment of history. At the heart of the matter lies the Biblical conception of "a people that dwells alone, not considered one of the nations" (Numbers 23:9). This aloneness is not an end in itself—mere aloofness—but a separation for the sake of being *different*, the outward manifestation of an inner reality expressed in the Bible as "you shall be holy" and in modern terms as "being yourself." Distinguishing oneself from others does not necessarily mean estrangement, and certainly not hatred. Rather, it means emphasizing and concentrating on what is distinct in oneself. Thus the relationship does not turn on "what the others will say about us" or even on "what we think of them," but on what we think of ourselves and do to actualize that potential. The Torah defined Israel's role among the nations as a priestly one: "You shall be to Me a kingdom of priests" (Exodus 19:6) for the world as a whole. It is the priest's responsibility, indeed reason to being, to devote himself, more than other men do, to the divine service. The responsibility is weighty, entailing demarcation in dress and deportment and, even more important, a focusing of attention on certain matters at the expense of others. It is not just a question of rising above unworthy concerns, but of steering clear of involvements that may be intrinsically worthwhile but are incompatible with the priestly role.

Another aspect to this apartness deals less with the inherent demands of the role than with the temptation to go astray and the need for barriers against that temptation. Even a people that is geographically concentrated is subject to alien influences; how much more so the people Israel, widely dispersed and in constant relations with others.

Woe to the person who defines himself in terms of others' rejection of him. Likewise, a group of people whose whole identity hinges on being hated: such a group has no real life of its own. Authentic selfhood can only be preserved by drawing boundaries and setting limits from within. Both the collective and the individual Jewish selves are continually threatened by alien involvement. And since such involvement is not always consciously perceived, it necessitates constant vigilance. In a general way, the vision of Israel as a "light unto the nations" is to be realized, not by preaching or missionizing, but by *being*, by serving as an example. It is by glowing, rather than any direct effort to kindle other lights, that Israel's task is to be accomplished.

This fundamental principle, of self-definition and distinctiveness, has wide-ranging practical and intellectual implications, from halakhic limitations on social contact to ways of relating to literature and culture, broadly conceived. *Kashrut*, though it has a hidden, intrinsic justification of its own, is one of the halakhic structures that serves to establish social boundaries. It forces the Jew to be circumspect, even among those closest to him. Another such device is the prohibition against *yayin nesekh* ("the wine of libation"), which has been extended from wine actually used in idolatrous ritual to all wine and wine derivatives (such as cognac) made or even touched by gentiles. (This prohibition does not apply to other beverages, even alcoholic ones.) Similarly, the prohibition against eating certain kinds of meat has been extended to include *bishulei nokhrim*—most food cooked by gentiles, either in utensils belonging to them or in Jewish utensils but without Jewish supervision, even when the ingredients are kosher.

The effect and purpose of all these restrictions is to create a certain social barrier. As the Sages said, "Their oil was prohibited because of [its association with] their wine, and their wine because of [its association with] their daughters." The severe prohibition against mixed marriage, repeated over and over again in the Torah, cannot be upheld where there is free social mingling, unhampered by any barriers. The idea is not to restrict Jews' ties with non-Jews, even on the level of deep friendship, let alone on a casual, collegial, or neighborly basis. In ancient times, when anti-Semitism was less common, many Jews, even among the Sages, had close gentile friends. Recognizing the existence of barriers, however, is the very thing that makes close contact possible. In fact, it is not always easy to maintain such complex relationships, based simultaneously on proximity and distance; yet this is one of the pillars of Jewish life wherever Jews and non-Jews live together.

Remaining distinct while mingling, being "a people that dwells alone" while not, in fact, dwelling alone, sums up the problem of Jews' social relations with the non-Jewish environment at every level. Our prophets enjoin us to be loyal to the polities within which we live, as long as we are allowed to maintain our Jewish life. Loyalty here means not just a passive inoffensiveness that keeps our safe haven intact; it means active participation in and identification with the life of the larger society. It is not just the halakhic rule of deferring to the law of the land (*dina demalkhuta dina*) which must guide a Jew's behavior, but a deeper sense of connectedness with and concern about the place in which he lives. This indeed is the pattern that Jewish leaders have tried to follow in all those countries that have granted Jews citizenship, even in countries with a checkered history in this regard. At the same time, involvement in the larger society must not detract from the sense of Jewish distinctiveness and commitment. The Jewish circle represents the innermost circle of life, the primary frame of reference, much like that of the family in its primacy. Jewish ties do not rule out other kinds of social connections any more than family ties do, but they do take precedence.

One of the most pressing issues is that of the spiritual and intellectual influence of the external environment, an issue that exists at least as much in *Eretz Yisrael* as in the Diaspora. Such influence is not limited to the realm of abstract ideas, but permeates every aspect of culture down to the most mundane details of everyday speech, behavior, and style. One cannot live within or alongside a culture without in some way coming to terms with it. Taken by itself, social intercourse, even of a very close personal nature, is a value-neutral undertaking in which people can come together despite differences in outlook. Cultural interaction, however, has definite value implications, though these may not always be evident at first glance. It is here that Jewish distinctiveness must be guarded most carefully and Jewish "aloneness" insisted upon, not just as a means of collective self-preservation but as a fact of collective identity.

One must remember that there *is*, in fact, a Jewish culture, different from all others. That is not to say that it must be sealed off from all contact with the outside world. Much has been borrowed from other cultures: vocabulary, scientific and technical achievements, etc. But such borrowing must be done consciously and with a critical eye. Many of the social and familial difficulties, and even more of the spiritual problems confronted by the contemporary Jew, can be traced to the considerable influence alien culture has upon his thinking. When the underlying values of that culture are at odds with those of the Jewish culture he carries within him, and when such contradictions are not recognized, they can lead to a whole chain of conflicts, distortions, and falsifications.

The phenomenon is not a new one, but it is heightened by the power and pervasiveness of contemporary media of communication. Today, no Jew can be completely oblivious to the surrounding environment; the only differences between one Jew and another are in their ways of responding to it. Even the person raised within and socially confined to a Jewish milieu must contend with external influences; how much more so the *ba'al teshuvah*, whose point of departure is on the outside. In his case it becomes essential to forge a *new* relationship with the non-Jewish environment, one based upon a recognition of the distinction between the two worlds, on drawing a line between "ours" and "theirs." Not all things non-Jewish are to be considered invalid or forbidden, but they must now be deemed acceptable according to Jewish criteria. The same constant vigilance one learns to exercise concerning the *kashrut* of the food imbibed by the body must be applied to the ideas imbibed by the soul. A Jewish pattern of life, not to mention a Jewish outlook, cannot be maintained when the heart and mind are indiscriminately open to everything that comes along. Nor can the world be completely kept out. The only solution is an ongoing process of selective incorporation.

The danger lies not only in the realm of explicit principles and beliefs—these are relatively easy to resist—but also in subtler, often unstated, underlying value-assumptions. A seemingly meaningless pattern of behavior, such as feeding the family dog or catching the 7:15 bus, can have important implications. Most people do not concern themselves very much with ideologies or abstractions, but they do give expression to the implicit world-view of their culture in everything they say and do—in their interaction with each other, in their work, in what they read, etc. A full-fledged Jewish commitment requires constant, conscious reexamination of accepted ideas and ways, one's own and others'. For lack of such reexamination, the gradual, often imperceptible accretion of alien or contradictory impulses will eventually lead to crisis.

In this selective encounter with the outside world, the Jew hears a warning sounded over and over in his own mind: these things are alien to me and inimical to what I stand for, and though I may find use in them, I must refrain from accepting them as they are. Such consciousness does not make for an easy way of life, particularly when the exposure to the alien must be sustained over a long period of time; but Jewish life has never been easy, anywhere, at any time. All people strive to preserve their integrity; the Jew makes of the effort a high art.

As for the *ba'al teshuvah*, his task is doubly difficult. While he may succeed in making a rapid transition from one cultural

framework to another—in itself not an easy accomplishment—
he must still reckon with the residue of his entire previous life.
He may think that by moving from one place to another or
changing his mode of dress he will avoid such problems; indeed,
these changes can be helpful in breaking with the past. But
ultimately they are only a veneer, and beneath the surface per-
sists an entire world of beliefs, knowledge, language, and behavior likely to conflict with the newly adopted Jewish pattern.
There is no way to deal with this dilemma except to become
closely involved in an authentic Jewish community, to study
and immerse oneself in Jewish values, and to work at rejecting
(or adapting) the alien elements. In this unending labor lies the
only hope of completing the transition once it has begun.

$=13=$

The Observant Community

As the *ba'al teshuvah* gets closer to Judaism, he also tends to move from relative isolation to greater contact with religious people. Such contact is, of course, not completely new to him—he has met observant Jews before, in the family, at work, or elsewhere—but these encounters have never been personally meaningful for him until now, when he himself is trying to become one of them. Now, too, the contact tends to take place not in religiously neutral settings, but in the framework of religious study, formal worship, and the like, where, again, it has an entirely different character. There is a new feeling of involvement and commonality, and the people themselves are seen in a much clearer, more realistic light. No longer are they stereotyped figures seen from a distance, but flesh-and-blood men and women. This contact has the greatest significance for him.

Sometimes the encounter between the *ba'al teshuvah*—the "new person"—and the traditional society to which he is seeking admission goes easily. Though he comes from another world and has a completely different upbringing, education, and life experience, he may yet feel very close to the people around him.

Sometimes it is a matter of hitting upon a community that is spiritually congenial to him. In such cases, the sense of closeness may be felt immediately and all the differences seemingly dispelled in the first few moments. There are times when the feeling is one of homecoming, of a return to the ancestral abode, or of discovering within oneself, as if long suppressed, the qualities one sees displayed around him—a return to one's true self. With time, this kind of encounter leads to a stronger and stronger bond, the differences and barriers fall away, and the *ba'al teshuvah* becomes truly a member of the community. Even partial integration is not necessarily a source of disappointment, but may, on the contrary, serve as an incentive to strive further.

In many instances, however, the encounter with the observant community is fraught with disappointment and pain. Such a "turn-off" may discourage the newcomer from pursuing his Jewish quest any further. If people raised on Judaism turn out like this, he may ask himself, why try to get any closer to it? The disillusionment may take different forms. The observant Jews the *ba'al teshuvah* meets, while being quite punctilious about certain *mitzvot*, may flagrantly violate others. A particular businessman, for example, may wear a beard and *pe'ot*, yet turn out to be dishonest in his business dealings, circumventing or deliberately violating the law and even cheating outright. Theft, fraud, and trickery are not unknown among observant Jews, and the fact that a man prays three times a day and puts on an extra pair of *tefillin* does not prevent him from being a scoundrel. A religious lawyer or worker is not necessarily a more reliable one. The dishonesty may extend even to trade in sacred objects. Nor is sexual immorality unheard of in religious circles. When the *ba'al teshuvah* discovers all this, he may well come to the conclusion that religious people, with their lofty pronouncements, are no better than the irreligious who do not pretend to special virtue.

Another shock awaiting the *ba'al teshuvah* is the abuses specifically connected with religion itself. In the synagogue, for example, he may find a petty and vicious rivalry over honors and responsibilities; quarreling and divisiveness that, however noble the cause, take an ugly turn; and a struggle for recognition, even by the esteemed and important, involving intrigue and character assassination. Along comes a person for whom the Jewish world is all sweetness and light, only to discover that there are factions and cliques, parties and personality clashes. Not only do the inhabitants of this world seem unable to get along with one another but, speaking in the name of Judaism, they desecrate the name of God and sully their own souls. Many synagogues and houses of study also leave a great deal to be desired aesthetically; in fact, they may be positively ugly, filled with cheapness and kitsch, littered and dirty. This too offends the sensibilities of the *ba'al teshuvah*.

The third and deepest disappointment of all is in the discovery that observant Jews—the "bearers and keepers of the Torah"—are themselves frequently not really interested in Torah! The *ba'al teshuvah* hears the idle talk in the synagogue and sees the neglect of *mitzvot* both great and small, even in the narrow realm of ritual. He finds that many of the people he has met in the synagogues and *batei midrash* lack any inner feeling for either prayer or study, and treat these as rote observances. He finds an alarming degree of ignorance about Judaism itself. Many of the men look like "rabbis" but turn out to be empty of either knowledge or interest in knowing more than they do. The world of the observant is, all too often, a hollow one, devoid of fervor, learning, or even faith.

Naturally, such discoveries are profoundly unsettling. Yet one must not get carried away with them so that one loses his sense of proportion. One must remember, for example, that the religious community is made up of all kinds of people. The *ba'al teshuvah* is by definition the product of a certain kind of self-selection. One does not undertake a massive redirection of one's life without a high degree of motivation, in this case, a strong attraction to Judaism. Such is not necessarily the case with Jews born into observant families. It is true that many of them, in some places the majority, are conscious and wholehearted in their commitment. But for others, the Jewish way of life is simply a matter of inheritance, which they are too lazy to cast aside or to which they have not found a satisfying alternative. Religious Jews, in other words, are an *unselected* group, in their views, their modes of behavior, and their levels of observance. One finds among them the whole range of types—honest and dishonest, scrupulous and unscrupulous—to be found in any other unselected population. Thus, generalizing about them on the basis of a few unpleasant experiences is hasty and misleading.

At the same time, one may legitimately ask how religious observance seems to have had no positive effect on these people, how all the time they have spent in the world of Judaism has not made them better people than they are. In fact, observance usually does have a profound effect on those who adhere to it—witness the negative change in behavior common among those who leave the religious life—but it is not the only factor which determines their personalities. Moral flaws exhibited by a religious individual simply reflect the inability of religion to overcome these qualities inherent in his character, not religion's lack of effect upon him. Indeed, were it not for the restraining influence of religion, might he not be a much worse person?

The *ba'al teshuvah* is one who undergoes a deep spiritual change, in the course of which the demands of faith, observance, and communal life take on a peculiar intensity. His fervor tends to be extreme, and it can distort his judgment of the people around him whose religiosity is a matter of long-established habit and, as a rule, less passionate. The *ba'al teshuvah* cannot always appreciate this difference between himself and the others. A similar comparison can be made between long- and short-distance runners: there is a difference not only in the duration of the course but also in the pace and style that are appropriate in each case. So too does the way of the fervent newcomer to religion differ from that of the person who has been immersed in it his whole life. Eventually the *ba'al teshuvah* discovers his own limitations and becomes aware that an entire life devoted to observance calls for a different "pace" and a different level of intensity. Only in rare cases—a few special individuals in each generation—can the initial fervor be maintained all through life. Ordinary people "slow down" and develop stable habits to take the place of their early flashes of enthusiasm.

An ongoing Jewish life must take into account a host of external and internal factors, including conditions that may be far from ideal. Often painful compromises must be made between the demands of the soul, the family, and the surrounding society. A person who has already made such compromises and worked out a pattern for himself may seem to be lacking in religious feeling, but one must not be too quick to judge him. Chances are he has arrived at his way of life after a long period of struggle, of learning, of trial and error. And often those who outwardly seem devoid of passion achieve greater spiritual heights than those whose zeal is more obvious and less tempered.

Most important of all, the *ba'al teshuvah* must learn *ahavat Yisrael*, the love of fellow-Jews, be they observant or not. Like all love, *ahavat Yisrael* cannot be reserved for those without blemish. In fact, such saintly Jews do exist, more than it is generally assumed; fortunate is the one who can find his way to them. But love demands something far more difficult; to see the flaws and yet forgive. A saint once explained the verse, "Hate not thy brother in thy heart," (Leviticus 19:17) to mean "Hate not thy brother, in that thy heart is bigger than his." One who is ready for such love, who is willing to accept his fellow-Jews for all their weaknesses, often discovers more good in them than he would otherwise have noticed.

PART II

═ 14 ═

Talmud Torah

The *mitzvah* of *talmud Torah*—Torah study—is a fundamental precept of Judaism. The Sages tell us that the Torah is one of the three things the world rests on, and that "the study of Torah outweighs all the other *mitzvot*" in importance and in the reward attached to it. A deeper understanding of this *mitzvah* requires that we distinguish between its two aspects, one within the other. The study of Torah is, first, the way that *knowledge* of Torah in all its dimensions—theoretical and practical, abstract and concrete—is acquired. It is through such study that one obtains guidance for life. It is through such study alone that one attains knowledge of Judaism itself.

The study of Torah also has another, inward aspect to it: it is itself a *mitzvah* and an important one, not only a means but also an end, an act that is inherently meaningful regardless of its practical consequences. The study of Torah is not a matter of learning "about" Judaism, but is in itself one of Judaism's essential components. Just as every *mitzvah*-fulfilling act derives meaning from the link it creates between the doer and the Giver of that *mitzvah*, so too does *talmud Torah* establish a connection between the learner and the Source of the text. Torah is both a gateway leading into the palace of Judaism and a great hall within that palace.

Being both means and end makes the study of Torah doubly obligatory. (For the details of women's obligation to learn Torah, see Chapter 21.) True, the Torah is "longer than the length of the earth and wider than the sea" (Job 11:9), and it is rare to attain mastery over more than a few of its many aspects. Nevertheless, no Jew is free of the obligation to study it to the best of his ability. The Jewish notion of "a kingdom of priests and a holy nation" rests to no small degree on the fact that Jewish knowledge is not restricted to a separate learned caste but incumbent upon all. One need not become a *talmid hakham* (i.e., achieve the pinnacle of scholarship), but he must not remain an *am ha-aretz* (ignoramus) either. The mountains of *halakhah*, the sea of the Talmud, and the vast plain of Jewish thought loom beyond the ordinary person like a terrain he cannot hope to traverse, particularly if he has not given the best years of his youth to this kind of study. Nonetheless, he is expected to learn what he can, to go as far as his abilities will carry him. Those ignorant of Torah have always been regarded as fundamentally deficient, however devoted they may have been as Jews, and however distinguished they may have been in other ways. Of course, ignorance is not always easy to remedy—the material or spiritual resources may be lacking—but this is no excuse for not trying. Indeed, over the ages, unlearned Jews have usually tried to learn, or at least to educate their children. Ignorance was never a state to which people simply resigned themselves.

One taking up Judaism is always in danger of accepting his own lack of knowledge or of contenting himself with bits and pieces, thus remaining an *am ha-aretz*. But the danger implied in the saying, "The ignorant man cannot fear sin, nor can the *am ha-aretz* be pious" applies with special severity to the *ba'al teshuvah*. Jews today tend to be highly educated in the secular realm, while their religious knowledge is spotty and superficial. This disproportion finds its reflection in a glaring imbalance in the soul. Judaism becomes for them a set of rituals grounded in superstition and nothing more. For the person coming to Judaism voluntarily as a result of personal effort and struggle, study is vital.

The newcomer's studies may at first be concentrated in a single area of Jewish learning that he finds particularly meaningful or helpful to gain entry to the realm of Judaism as a whole. But it is important for him to see these first efforts as only an introduction to a longer and much broader course of study, encompassing all the various aspects of Torah. In Torah study, as elsewhere, there is a dialectical relation between objective demands and personal affinities; some plausible path must be sought between the two. One must keep in mind the distinction between experience and knowledge. Someone whose knowledge is meager can get quite excited over what little he knows, and his excitement can spur him on in his religious development; yet his knowledge may remain rudimentary. There are, of course, people with a special gift for picking out the essentials, who can master a few truly fundamental things and build an entire religious life on them. But generally a little knowledge means fragmented, one-sided, incorrect knowledge. What is "known" may be marvelously interesting, but also largely a product of the "knower's" own imagination, bearing little relation to the Torah of Israel. Thus it is not only those who are misinformed or underinformed who need to study, but also those who have known religious experience, who are in need of the balance and the perspective on their experience that real knowledge can provide.

To a certain extent, the mode of study is even more important than its content. For example, an essential element, no matter the subject matter, is *regularity*, an inflexible commitment to the study of particular subjects at particular times and in particular places. It is this regularity, among other things, that prevents Torah study from turning into mere dilletantism or intellectual entertainment. Regularity gives such study the quality of an almost professional regimen, however little time is devoted to it and however low the level of inquiry may be. Flipping pages whenever it is convenient to do so may be a pleasant pastime, but it has little to do with serious learning. Are we not enjoined to make of the study of Torah something more than a hobby?

Another part of the "how-to" of Torah study concerning finding others to learn with, at least some of the time. The Sages speak at length about this question, and are emphatic about the virtues of studying together as well as the pitfalls of studying alone. In their view, even a partner whose knowledge does not exceed one's own is preferable to no partner at all. Of course, joint study is extremely helpful in maintaining regularity, for which most of us, left alone, do not have adequate self-discipline. Studying with others also tends to create a social bond that can become quite deep. But even if it does not, a certain mutual reinforcement takes place. Most important of all, there is the corrective role partners can play for each other in the course of study. Everyone, particularly the beginner, if left to his own devices, runs the risk of misunderstanding or distorting what he learns, of seeing the material through his own idiosyncratic perspective. Even people of superior intelligence run this risk. But study partners can serve as a kind of check against each other's subjectivity.

Far more important is finding a teacher, someone more knowledgeable, from whom one can learn. A teacher's importance often goes beyond the assistance provided in study per se; a teacher can serve as a mentor, master, and guide well beyond those confines. Indeed, finding such a person is likely to be a decisive turning point in the learner's life. But even the teacher who is less than a mentor can provide something more than mere technical assistance. Every teacher worthy of the name supplements the text, provides context, and fills in between the lines. This added insight may be unavailable in any book. This is what the Sages had in mind when they said that "serving the [teachers of] Torah is better than studying it." The things one picks up in passing, the things that cannot be transmitted verbally, are often the most important, and it may be only much later that one realizes how important they were. Thus, even if a master cannot be found, one should find a teacher; and even if a teacher cannot be found, one should find at least one study partner, particularly if one happens to be a beginner on the Jewish path.

Just to avoid being an *am ha-aretz* and to be a reasonably literate Jew (*yode'a sefer*), not to mention a scholar or teacher, one must learn an enormous amount. Even a person who has set aside time for concentrated study in an institutional framework is likely to find that he must supplement his study, outside the classroom, just to reach the level of knowledge acquired without any apparent effort by those born and raised in a Jewish environment. Still, a beginning has to be made somewhere, and once a basis has been acquired, it can be built on. One should, as the Sages say, study what one's heart desires with whomever one's heart desires. The larger body of Jewish knowledge is objectively defined, but each person must approach it in his own way. As the Sages put it: "Just as their faces are all different, so are their minds all different." Subject matter in which one person finds the answers to all his deepest questions can leave another cold.

One sort of knowledge that is essential is the language of the sources, especially the Hebrew language, even if that knowledge be nothing more than passive comprehension. Nor is a command of modern conversational Hebrew sufficient; the older language found in the sources differs not only in its antiquity but also in its inner logic. True, one can attain a certain understanding of Judaism through translations of the basic texts (and most of them are available in translation), but history teaches us that a reliance on "Judaism in translation" is perilous both for Jewish communities and for individual Jews. The existence of an impenetrable technical barrier to understanding tends to give rise to a new spiritual life with an ersatz basis, a kind of "second-hand Judaism." Hence the importance of sufficient knowledge of Hebrew.

It is very important to know the Bible, if possible in its entirety. What is essential is the knowledge, not of obscure details, but of the overall contents of the various books, the themes and stories. It is desirable to learn certain chapters by heart. And it should be kept in mind that, while the study of the Bible can be a lifelong task, every literate person is capable of reading it through several times, with or without the help of translations or commentaries, and acquiring a basic mastery in a relatively short time. The *Humash* (Pentateuch) is, of course, covered once each year in the cycle of weekly public readings in the synagogue. But the reading there is too fast to be fully comprehensible, and it is desirable, indeed obligatory, to read each weekly portion on one's own, "twice in the original and once in translation." Here, the ruling that Rashi's commentary qualifies as a "translation" is a good one to take advantage of. These weekly exercises provide a recurring opportunity to deepen one's knowledge of the text, and, linked as they are to the calendar and the rhythm of communal observance, they also contribute to the regularity of one's studies.

Another important area of study is *halakhah*. Here, the difference in level between the true scholar and the beginner is quite pronounced. Yet there is a wide-ranging introductory literature in a number of languages that provides access to the subject, at almost any level. Here too *halakhah* itself offers guidance as to how one should proceed: begin with the laws of everyday observance, such as those of prayer, *Shabbat*, *kashrut*, and *tahorat hamishpahah*. After learning just enough of these laws to avoid transgressing them unwittingly, go back and study them in a more systematic way.

Some people find it helpful to pore over modern legal digests, such as the *Kitzur Shulhan Arukh*, which supply the practical do's and dont's incumbent on a Jew. These books do not deal with rationales or underlying principles, so they should be seen only as handbooks. While reading through such a book once or twice is unlikely to give one mastery of all the thousands of details it contains, at least one will have an awareness of the problems and where to look initially for their solution. Indeed, these are the real purposes of these books.

For others, reading dry halakhic texts is wearisome and unproductive compared with an investigation of abstract principles. A number of more interestingly written books answer this need, leading the student by logical deduction through the otherwise overwhelming mass of halakhic information. Of course, the study of *halakhah* is not exhausted with an acquisition of general knowledge of what to do and where to go for practical guidance; but that is where the emphasis should be placed at first, however compelling other subjects may seem by comparison.

The Talmud and its commentaries represent another significant area of learning. Here, the differences between people at various levels of knowledge reflect not only the different amounts of time that have been devoted to study, but also different degrees of ability. In Talmud, a high level of mastery reflects a special talent, and one's achievements are not always proportional to one's efforts. Then, too, some people quickly discover in themselves an affinity for the Talmud and plunge into it with enthusiasm, while others never develop much interest. Nevertheless, the importance of the Talmud as a basic text for all aspects of Judaism is inestimable, and every Jew must have some familiarity and facility with it.

Ignorance of the Oral Torah (the Talmud) is more serious than ignorance of Scripture. A certain knowledge (even if it be minimal) of the Talmud constitutes a basis for almost all the other fields of Judaism, as all of them are directly or indirectly connected with it and continuously nurtured by it. Therefore, without any such minimal basic knowledge, all the other fields of Judaism are understood in a shallow and even incorrect manner. Furthermore, the study of Talmud is a discipline that gives balance to the spirit and restrains its more extreme proclivities. It is a "holy intellectualism," which can provide a sound anchorage for other kinds of spiritual exploration.

The study of Jewish mysticism, the Kabbalah, presents a special problem. Though the Kabbalah is probably the only extant Jewish theological system, there are various attitudes to its study, which question not the relative value of studying Kabbalah, but the qualifications necessary to undertake it. It is very important to recognize that, unlike other mystical doctrines, the Kabbalah is not a discipline unto itself but is closely linked to mainstream religious practice. It is in a sense a commentary on both the written and oral Torah, and cannot be separated either in theory or practice from the full panoply of the *mitzvot*.

There are relatively few places where Kabbalah can be studied properly, and the secondary literature available on the subject tends to be superficial, un-Jewish, or even anti-Jewish. While recent rabbinic authorities have ruled that study of "the doctrine of hidden things" need not be suppressed, it is nonetheless advisable to avoid getting into mysticism in an unbalanced way. One drawn to Judaism along the mystical path should take special pains to study *halakhah* as well, particularly the Talmud and its commentaries, both in order to better understand the Kabbalah itself—a connection a number of well-known scholars have underscored—and in order to keep one's balance and avoid going astray. It is false and misleading to view the Jewish mystical tradition apart from the larger context of Judaism as a whole.

Finally, there is the study of Jewish thought in all its many facets. The various schools differ more in their modes of expression than in their underlying ideas, which the student is likely to find repeated from one system to another. But, particularly for one just starting out, it is advisable to stay with a single approach as long as it answers one's questions and meets one's needs. Attempts to combine and synthesize various approaches often end in confusion and superficiality. Of course, one does not always find a congenial approach right away, so some experimentation may be necessary. But, if possible, it is better to understand one thing well than to glean tidbits simultaneously from too many diverse sources.

To repeat, Torah-study is not just a way of gaining entree to the other *mitzvot*, but a fundamental *mitzvah* in its own right, incumbent on every Jew as long as he lives. One must not rest content with "pious ignorance," but rather strive for real achievement in the realm of Jewish learning, in all its branches.

15

Prayer

Almost every *ba'al teshuvah* has to struggle at one time or another with prayer, and that struggle is often with himself as well. There are two aspects to this: On the one hand, prayer is a practical *mitzvah* to which time and attention must be devoted and that cannot be fulfilled by an occasional gesture alone. On the other hand, prayer is also not just a physical act to which one can attach whatever meaning one chooses, but rather it is a thing with specific objective contents to which one must somehow relate. To the person brought up in a religious environment, however thoughtful he may be, prayer is a matter of habit, indeed of second nature. The person approaching prayer as a new experience is much more aware of its content and form, his ear more alert to nuances of meaning, and his eye more likely to notice beauty and its opposite. But this very sensitivity can engender conflict and lead to alienation. Almost all beginners have trouble praying, though some have more and some less, and they have different kinds of difficulties. It is not unusual for one person's stumbling block to be another's inspiration.

The most immediate problem for many, if not all, beginners arises from the fact that, while other *mitzvot* are ways of getting closer to God, prayer represents a direct turning to Him. The very wording—"Thou, O Lord"—as well as the content of the liturgy imply both the possibility and the necessity of directly addressing the Divinity. But the worshipper may well ask himself, "Do I really believe what I am saying? Can I really speak to God?" Be it a prayer of thanksgiving, praise, or petition, there is a clear assumption of connectedness between human beings and God, and the person uttering the words may well ask himself whether this connectedness, this "Thou," is something he actually feels. The novice may interpret the very fact that he has this problem as evidence of a lack of faith or dedication. Yet it is a basic problem from which no religious person is exempt, unless he has exempted himself from questions of all kinds.

Only the privileged few can feel fully at one, heart and soul, with the words they utter in prayer. As for the general run of Jews, *"avodat hashem bitefilah,"* "the service of the Lord is in prayer," but that service is also hard "work," indeed lifelong labor (another meaning of *avodah*). A certain saint once said, "In my youth I longed to be able to say a single service properly. When I became more mature I prayed to be able to say a single benediction wholeheartedly. And when I went up to the Land of Israel, the air of which makes one wise, I realized that what I should have been asking for was the ability to utter a single word with sincerity." In other words, it is not only a problem for those approaching Judaism from afar, but also for those whose entire lives have been spent in a Jewish ambience and whose piety is the most exalted. Indeed, it is the nobler souls, with their heightened sensitivities, who may be most keenly troubled by a disparity between heart and lips.

Rather than forsaking prayer altogether, the troubled soul must come to see its meaning and function in a different way. To the extent that prayer involves petition, it must include a request for the ability to pray itself. To the extent that prayer is a *mitzvah*, it is something that, like other *mitzvot*, one learns by doing. It is by actually praying that one finds a way to pray properly. To say "Blessed art Thou, O Lord" is to turn directly to the living presence of God, but it is also to ask that He *be* present, that He reveal Himself, so that the prayer that follows may be sincerely addressed to Him. To pray is also, at the same time, to ready oneself for prayer. The words one utters do not just come from the heart but also act upon it.

The "service of the heart" (*avodat halev*), which is the essence of prayer, is not confined to prayer but informs every aspect of the life of a religious Jew. As a person proceeds along the path of religious growth, he frequently discovers that the words he has been saying with conviction were only superficially understood. In order to pray he must then reappropriate the language of the prayers at a higher level of understanding. This is a recurring problem, endemic in the situation of prayer, and it must not be allowed to inhibit the worshipper from praying at all. He may, indeed must, continue to pray as long as he has some insight into what he is saying. If at bottom he is engaged in the sincere expression of what his heart feels, the lingering questions and doubts can be tolerated. Part of worship is in the preparation. A gap may still exist between human beings and God, but narrowing that gap is the work of a lifetime and not something to be accomplished all at once.

The specific content of the liturgy also, in many cases, poses a problem for the beginner. Prayers that seem to have meaning for those around him may appear to him alien and irrelevant. A particular prayer may give expression to something he does feel, while the next prayer may not speak for him at all. Or a prayer that seemed meaningful in one set of circumstances may cease to have meaning in another. The prayer for healing inevitably means less to one who is well than to one who is ill, and the prayer for sustenance has more immediate significance to a poor person than to one who is rich. Rarely can one relate personally to all the prayers in a given service.

A partial solution to this problem may be found in a deeper understanding of the liturgy itself. Significantly, most Jewish prayer is couched in the first person plural rather than the first person singular. It is not, on the whole, personal, individual prayer, but collective prayer, the prayer of the whole House of Israel. Consequently, it includes in its concerns all the diverse problems and needs, feelings and aspirations to be found in the Jewish community as a whole. Each person prays, not only for himself, but for everyone. Thus we find in the teachings of the Ari (the great Kabbalist Rabbi Yitzhak Luria), as well as in a number of *siddurim*, the injunction to begin one's prayers with a commitment to *ahavat Yisrael*, the love of Israel—that is, with a renewed identification with the Jewish people.

Because Jewish prayer is the prayer of the people as a whole, the times set for it correspond to those set for public worship—the sacrificial rites in the Temple in Jerusalem—in ancient times. To some extent there is even a correspondence in the internal structure of the services. It is in this sense too that our prayers may be considered *avodah*, "service" in the original sacrificial sense. Even the outward gestures accompanying such prayers as the *Shmoneh-Esreh*—the nineteen benedictions said silently in a standing position during each of the weekday services—suggest the Temple rite: stepping from the outer "to the inner chambers, standing in awe before God in the Holy of Holies, bowing at the utterance of certain words, withdrawing. The prescribed direction of prayer too—toward the Land of Israel; once there, toward Jerusalem; once there, toward the Temple Mount (a pattern expressed somewhat differently in Solomon's prayer in Kings 1:8)—is intended to reinforce the feeling that the people of Israel as a whole is turning toward the center of its life.

On the other hand, the collective character of the liturgy does not negate the value of distinctive, individual prayer. This can be done in two ways. One is by adding personal petitions, mentally or out loud, while reciting the *Shmoneh-Esreh*. Thus a particular sin can be the focus of the regular prayer for forgiveness, or a particular illness the focus of the prayer for healing. Petitions that do not fall under any of the other benedictions can be subsumed under *shema kolenu*, the general benediction beginning "Hear our voice." Some *siddurim* actually provide formulas for such insertions, but these are not binding. It is permissible to add whatever one wishes. In addition, personal prayer is appropriate whenever and wherever one feels the need, be it in the synagogue or elsewhere, and whatever the language or mode of address. There have even been groups of Jews who have set aside particular times for such prayer, times when one might "speak with the Holy One, blessed be He" and pour out one's heart to Him. This kind of prayer, arising from individual situations, does not conflict with the established, collective liturgy but rather complements it.

The liturgy reflects the sentiments and needs of the House of Israel as a whole, and all are summoned to take part in it; yet there is room for each person's individuality as well.

Another kind of difficulty arises from the *length* of the liturgy, particularly *Shaharit*, the morning service. Though the text itself is not very long, the person new to the practice of regular prayer tends, in his heightened sensitivity, to want to dwell on the words, and this in turn can draw out greatly the time required to complete the service. Those who feel this need, yet who are under time constraints, are permitted to recite an abbreviated version of the service—just the benedictions before the *Shema*, the *Shema* itself, and the *Shmoneh-Esreh*—and gradually add the rest of the service as time permits. It is also natural for the beginner to want to concentrate on those prayers that are especially meaningful for him, and within limits (as long as it does not become a fixed practice) this is permissible as well as sensible. However, it is important to remember that the service is not just an arbitrary piling up of things but a carefully articulated structure, put together with attention to detail and to the interrelation of the parts. Both the components themselves and the order in which they are connected have an esoteric significance as well as a calculated emotional effect.

While the richness of the content, the great number of themes requiring thoughtful attention, is the main source of frustration with the lengthiness of Jewish prayer, there is another source as well: its repetitiveness. The structure of the service and its various components—the *Shmoneh-Esreh*—remain more or less constant from morning to afternoon to evening, from day to day, from month to month. Thus, instead of being an uplifting, inspiring experience, prayer can come to seem like a mere routine, dry and tiresome. This problem, which the Sages refer to as the draining of the element of "supplication before the Almighty" from fixed prayer, is felt by every observant Jew, but it is likely to be experienced with particular keenness by someone unused to the regularity of prayer. The accepted remedy is *iyun tefilah*, conscious inquiry into the deeper meaning of the text, its language and themes, so as to arrive at a fresh perspective upon it. Initial exposure to a particular prayer or service—or exposure that comes only infrequently, as with the High Holy Day liturgy—makes a strong impression on the worshipper, akin to the experience of seeing a beautiful landscape for the first time or witnessing an unusual event. But the freshness of the first-time experience inevitably fades; then it is time for a more probing look. From a largely passive, emotional encounter one turns to a more active, more thoughtful, more strenuous engagement and appropriation.

These dynamics are not confined to the realm of prayer. Similar observations could be made about religious practice in general and, indeed, about many other areas of life. The things we experience and do fall into two fundamental categories: the new and unusual and the regular and habitual. The first involves strong impressions and reactions, the second more moderate effects. Life is never confined to either one realm or the other. We are incapable of living in a permanent state of excitation. When a deluge of powerful experiences overloads our capacity to absorb them, we simply turn off part of our sensitivity. But a wholly routinized life, too, is intolerable and leads in its own way to a dulling of the senses.

The part of our lives that involves repetition and constancy has to be seen as a kind of backdrop, a setting of order and quiet, against which dramatic or meaningful events transpire. In the religious realm, that backdrop is supplied by the regular pattern of observance, including the fixed liturgy and the round of daily prayer. This pattern gives life a much-needed rhythmical quality, as regards both action and perception. Yet against this backdrop, room for innovation and emotion still exist. The "institutionalization" implicit in a fixed way of life provides a stable basis for higher, but more precarious, kinds of experience. One who insists on continual novelty at all costs foregoes the opportunity to examine, integrate, and deepen his relationship to what he has experienced. He risks being dazzled by the superficial brilliance of each new revelation and never achieves the inner illumination that comes only with familiarity. The Sages tell us to "see [the words of the Torah] afresh each day." What they mean, then, is that we must struggle consciously and continuously to find the new within the old.

16

Shabbat

The observance of the Sabbath is one of the most important precepts of Judaism. The holiness of the day and the
commandments to remember and honor it are stressed
throughout the sources, from the description of the Creation,
in which *Shabbat* plays a central role, to the Ten Commandments, the Latter Prophets and Hagiographa, and subsequent
Jewish literature of every age and locale. Illuminating testimony
to the unique stature of *Shabbat* in Jewish tradition can also be
seen in the fact that in Hebrew it is the only day of the week
with a proper name, while the other days are named in relation
to it: "the first day of [the week ending in] *Shabbat*," "the second day . . . ," etc.

As great as *Shabbat* is, so too are the difficulties that stand
in the way of one who would observe it properly and experience
it fully without having been raised in its observance. It is not,
after all, merely a once-a-year celebration, but something that
must be reckoned with each and every week. What is more, it
is a day overflowing with laws and customs that impinge greatly
upon one's usual ways of behaving, even thinking. Hence a

great deal of effort is required if *Shabbat* is to be made a part of one's life.

The Jewish Sabbath is unique. Indeed, a comparison with the Christian and Muslim imitations of it—not to mention the modern secular "weekend"—only underlines this uniqueness. *Shabbat* is not simply a day when one refrains from work, nor is it merely the day when it is customary to attend public prayer. It is a day when one enters a completely different sphere. The rabbinic sayings comparing *Shabbat* to the world to come are more than mere figures of speech. Basically, *Shabbat* means putting aside creative activity in order to concern oneself completely with personal reflection and matters of the spirit, free of struggle and tension. The key element in *Shabbat* observance is a kind of passivity: refraining from "work." Yet, over a period of three thousand years, the Jewish people have developed a tradition that transforms what might otherwise be a day of mere inactivity into one of joy and inner peace, "a day of rest and holiness," in the words of the liturgy. This tradition is one of the hallmarks of Jewish culture as a whole.

Approached from a distance, the body of *Shabbat* prohibitions can appear to be an endless maze of details: "don't do," "don't move," "don't touch." Yet for all the elaboration these prohibitions have received, the principles underlying them are actually quite simple. The key formula here is, "Thou shalt not do any manner of *melakhah*." The concept of *melakhah* is understood both in the simple sense of "work," which is its plain meaning, and in the more complex sense that flows from the context in which it first appears, the story of the Sabbath of Creation. In the latter case, the term has the meaning of *an act of physical creation*. What is decisive is not the degree of effort involved, or whether the action receives monetary compensation, but rather whether it results in the appearance of something new in the physical world. Thus, relatively effortless activities like writing and profitless activities like landscaping one's house become forbidden. Similarly, it is not permitted to kindle or handle fire on *Shabbat*, a fact that has always been of great practical significance. Not only is smoking prohibited; so is operating a vehicle or tool requiring internal combustion.

Over and above the basic prohibitions, a set of secondary restrictions was enacted by the Rabbinical authorities down through the ages. A few of these laws were in effect as early as the period of the First Temple. These are known as *shevut* prohibitions. In most cases they are intended as a hedge around the more fundamental prohibitions, designed to prevent certain habitual activities from leading to *Shabbat* violations. Such activities include commerce, playing musical instruments, taking drugs (unless they are vital), riding animals (a prohibition also based on the positive Biblical injunction to allow animals to rest on *Shabbat*), and handling *muktseh* objects. The notion of *muktseh* is a complex one in *halakhah*, but basically it refers to objects the normal use of which entails an activity forbidden on *Shabbat*; raw materials (such as stone, soil, and wood) not prepared specifically for use on *Shabbat*; and especially money.

Two kinds of prohibitions derive from the general statement "Let no man leave his place on the seventh day" (Exodus 16:29). On the one hand, it is forbidden to go further than the boundary of the locality in which one lives (the *tehum Shabbat*); on the other hand, it is forbidden to take things out of one's house or to carry them about in public places (see Jeremiah 17:21-22). In Israel and in certain other countries, a "mingling of realms"—*eruv hatserot*—is often effected in a given locality (following special Rabbinical rulings on this subject).

The main principle underlying the *eruv* is the creation of a circumscribed area. The two central practices connected with it are the creation of a symbolic fence around a city (or any part of it) formed by an arrangement of posts and wire, and a symbolic communal meal shared by all those participating in the *eruv*. In large cities with main streets full of public traffic it becomes necessary to have an additional system of fences, which is not always possible to implement in practical or halachic terms. The *eruv* allows things to be carried almost anywhere within that locality. But this is not the case in most places in the Diaspora or even in certain places in Israel, and it is always best to ask knowledgeable local people how to deal with such practical problems as carrying keys, handkerchiefs, and prayerbooks on *Shabbat*.

The preceding is just an outline of *halakhah* on this subject, and much more detail needs to be learned, but all the rest is derived in one way or another from these basic principles. The upshot is that the only work that may be done on *Shabbat* is simple household tasks: picking up after oneself, light cleaning, and preparing meals (without cooking, baking, or readying raw food for use). It is permitted to cut and serve pre-prepared foods, or food that does not require manufacture (vegetable, fruit, etc.). Warm foods are permitted on the Sabbath when their preparation does not require ignition or changing the heat of the oven on the Sabbath itself. It is not only permitted to leave hot water for the Sabbath, but certain traditional Sabbath foods, like *cholent*, are dishes that are kept in the oven so they can be eaten hot. Otherwise, it is a day without ordinary activity, a day devoted to special things, "supplied with all that it needs" by the other days of the week.

In our own time, *Shabbat* observance has been made easier by the introduction of automatic timing devices ("*Shabbos* clocks") to turn electrical appliances on and off and thermostatically controlled heating elements for keeping food warm. These technological advances may be used because the *Shabbat* prohibitions apply, not to the processes themselves, but to the human performance of them. Still, there are numerous halakhic restrictions involved in the use of such devices. These details need to be mastered, and it is best to get practical advice from people more expert in such matters before making too many assumptions about what is permitted and what is not.

The heart of *Shabbat* observance is, as I have said, refraining rather than doing: cessation. But there is also the positive dimension of the "culture" of *Shabbat*, the dimension that makes it, in the words of the liturgy, "a day of joy and rest, quiet and security," a day of holiness, a day when one acquires an "extra soul."

Thus, before *Shabbat* begins, candles are lit, preferably on or near the dinner table. This practice, which was originally intended to make the Sabbath evening meal more enjoyable, has always had a festive quality to it: the brightness of the light gives added honor to the day. Every Jew is obliged to light candles, but over the centuries the tradition arose that it should be done, wherever possible, by the woman of the house. (There is also a beautiful custom according to which *each* female member of the family, even little girls, lights her own *Shabbat* candles). The connection between the night of *Shabbat* and the woman's role is a deep and ancient one, of which the candle-lighting is but one part.

Unlike weekday meals, those eaten on *Shabbat* are not for physical sustenance alone but serve to fulfill the mitzvah of Sabbath joy. It is also a *mitzvah* to eat three *Shabbat* meals: evening, noon, and late afternoon. These are "sacred meals," both in their ceremonial character and in their deeper meaning, meals in which the Jewish family, as a religious (and not merely social) unit, communes with the sanctity of the day. The first two of the three meals begin with *Kiddush* ("sanctification"), a special benediction usually said over a cup of wine (or spirits or grape juice in the case of people who do not tolerate alcohol well). After *netilat yadayim* (ritual hand washing), the meal itself begins. In most Jewish communities it is customary to sing *zemirot*, special Sabbath hymns, at the table. This custom is not restricted to people with special musical talents; rather, each person at the table participates as best he can. The effect is to reinforce both the sense of togetherness and the element of *zevah mishpahah*—familial offering—appropriate to the Sabbath table.

The solemnity of the *Shabbat* meals, and of *Shabbat* in general, should not be taken to imply heaviness or gloom, nor should the element of restriction be allowed to predominate. On the contrary, festivity is of the essence. Even one who is newly bereaved or has a fresh memory of some other personal catastrophe must stop mourning when *Shabbat* arrives. The *neshamah yeterah* ("extra soul") each Jew is said to acquire on *Shabbat* is really an augmented ability to rejoice in tranquillity, to cease doing things as if all were already done, to accept life with a feeling of wholeness and contentment. Not only is *Shabbat* a time to disengage oneself from workaday affairs—even reading, speaking, and thinking about them are forbidden—but when it comes to spiritual matters, too, vexation and anxious self-analysis should be avoided. The holiness of the day must be sought in a spirit of *oneg Shabbat* ("the joy of the Sabbath"), of pleasure, relaxation, and ease.

Shabbat should be devoted as much as possible to holy activities, which one may feel he has no free time for during the week, especially prayer and study. Thus, one who finds it inconvenient for one reason or another to attend public prayer during the week should make a special effort to do so on *Shabbat*. While the *mitzvot* of *Shabbat* also apply to isolated individuals, it is desirable to foster collective—familial and communal—observance of them. In addition, certain aspects of public worship, such as the ceremonial reading of the Torah, cannot be done alone. So while it may be a long walk to the nearest synagogue, and one may not find the people there entirely congenial, it is important to make the effort to join them. Of course, synagogue attendance is not nearly as important as *Shabbat* observance itself. Thus the person who rides to the synagogue, in serious violation of the Sabbath laws, in effect, sacrificed the principle of cessation from labor, which is the very basis of *Shabbat*, in favor of an observance of secondary significance.

It is appropriate to devote a certain amount of time each *Shabbat* to Torah study, if possible in communal and family settings. One may not be able to cover much ground in a once-a-week session, but the fulfillment of the *mitzvah* consists of setting aside a signficant block of time for spiritual nourishment rather than of any particular intellectual achievement. Other kinds of activities—a political discussion with friends, a game of chess—may be permissible on *Shabbat*, but they should not be allowed to predominate. Sport per se is not considered *melakhah*, but the Sages forbade certain more active kinds of athletic activity because their strenuousness was not in the spirit of *Shabbat*. Watching commercial sporting events is forbidden because such events usually entail many kinds of *hillul Shabbat* ("violation of the *Shabbat*")—traveling, buying tickets, etc.—and in public besides. In general, it is not play or free movement that is ruled out, but activity that involves strain and effort. The issue of play on *Shabbat* arises most acutely, of course, in the case of children, whose main source of pleasure involves jumping and running. Because for them as well, *Shabbat* should be a gift and not a burden, the halakhic authorities have long been lenient toward them in such matters.

A person raised on Sabbath observance can easily understand its spiritual dimension, but for the beginner the unaccustomed effort involved may obscure the day's inner meaning. Abstention from *melakhah*, with all its practical and social difficulties, may at first seem an almost intolerable burden. It might be best, then, to start with something symbolic—for example, lighting candles, an act that brings the beauty of *Shabbat* into the home in a visible way. Of course, they must be lit at the proper time (as indicated in Jewish calendars) and not, as sometimes happens, at the dinner table or in the synagogue long after *Shabbat* has already begun. The latter practice is a direct violation of *Shabbat* and a contradiction of its spirit and, as such, it cheapens the act of candle-lighting itself.

When one is ready, a further important step, and one with numerous ramifications, is to refrain from *hillul Shabbat* in *public*. Down through the ages the Sages have regarded such violations with extreme seriousness. *Shabbat* is in many ways the "banner" of the people of Israel. Thus, publicly trampling on it represents a rather dramatic statement of disidentification. By the same token, honoring the Sabbath in public is a kind of affirmation of solidarity. On a more personal level, too, whether or not one observes *Shabbat* makes a real difference to those around one. There are three ways of publicly honoring the day: refraining from work, refraining from travel, and refraining from smoking in public. The first has relatively few social consequences in Israel, where *Shabbat* is the official day of rest, and for most Jews in other countries with Monday to Friday work weeks. Yet even here there are changes to be made that others should be told about and to which they must learn to adapt. Most *ba'alei teshuvah* will have to take measures to begin the *Shabbat* at the appropriate time on Friday, particularly in the winter. Those who are called on, or accustomed, to work on Saturday may experience some initial difficulties in making alternative arrangements. Refraining from travel, too, has a social significance: the observer must find ways of spending the day close to home, and family ties and friendships are inevitably improved. Forms of recreation involving "going out" are sacrificed in favor of more positive, home-centered pastimes, and new companions are sought to share them.

Here, as in other aspects of *teshuvah*, married people are likely to have quite a different experience than single people. If one's spouse or family share in the process, they can make it much easier by providing mutual support; if they do not, if the *ba'al teshuvah* is isolated within his own home, the process can be much harder, for then he must both deal with the internal friction and seek companionship elsewhere.

Part of the impact of *Shabbat* observance on one's life is in the area of leisure time. When properly observed, *Shabbat* gives one time for a number of activities one might otherwise have been "too busy" for: being with family and friends, reading, etc. At the same time, one loses one night each week when one could stay out late, and one of the two days each week that could be devoted entirely to household chores, correspondence, strenuous recreation, or traveling. One must then find ways to squeeze these things in during weekdays, on Sundays, and during vacations. And if one lives in a locality where stores are closed on Sunday, one loses the weekly shopping day too. While such adjustments rarely cause real hardship, they demand effort and determination.

A final difficulty with *Shabbat* observance arises from one's friends and relatives, who continue to be non-observant and who often will try to be helpful by offering to serve as "*Shabbos goyim*," i.e., by offering to do things for the Sabbath-observer that are forbidden for him to do himself. As a rule, such offers must be declined, certainly never solicited; if help is given nonetheless, it is forbidden to benefit from it until after *Shabbat* is over. Even when the person offering is a gentile not subject to the *mitzvot* of *Shabbat*, such help is acceptable only in exceptional cases. Needless to say, help offered by a Jew that involves a *Shabbat* violation is to be rejected altogether. The observance of *Shabbat* is not merely a voluntary personal undertaking, but an obligation that applies to all Jews, whether they honor it or not.

As one progresses in the observance of *Shabbat*, there are numerous fine points to learn. For this purpose, it is helpful to visit observant friends who are more knowledgeable in such matters and to consult any of several available manuals of religious practice (see "Suggestions for Further Reading," p. 176). While *Shabbat's* enhancement of one's life invariably turns out to be greater than anticipated, the difficulty of observing it usually turns out to be less as one gains experience and learns to deal with the problems.

17

The Festivals

In a broad sense, the term *haggim* (festivals) applies to all the days of the year that have a festive character. But the term is used more narrowly to describe only the *yamim tovim* (singular: *yom tov*), holy days whose observance is expressly prescribed in the Torah. They include *Rosh Hashanah, Yom Kippur* (which, however, has a special status because of the fast and other observances), *Sukkot, Shemini Atzeret/Simhat Torah, Pesah,* and *Shavuot.* A second group of holy days, distinguished mainly by modifications of the liturgy and sometimes by other practices, was established by the Sages in post-Biblical times. The most important of the latter is *Rosh Hodesh* (the new moon).

While each of the *yamim tovim* has distinctive *mitzvot* and customs, they also have certain observances in common. They are days of cessation from what the Torah calls *melekhet avodah*—"labor," in a special sense—unlike *Shabbat,* when *kol melakhah*—"all labor"—is prohibited. (On *Yom Kippur,* referred to as the "Sabbath of Sabbaths," this stricter formulation also applies.) There is also a difference in the severity of the prohibition: desecrating *Shabbat* (and to a slightly lesser extent *Yom Kippur*) by labor is a very serious transgression, while the transgression is less serious in the case of *yom tov*. But this difference was largely nullified, in effect, by certain greater stringencies imposed on the *yamin tovim* by the Sages in order to underline the sanctity of these days.

The most obvious practical difference between *Shabbat* and the *yamin tovim* is that in the latter case we are permitted *melekhet okhel nefesh*—"labor necessary to prepare food." In practice, *halakhah* draws a line, permitting only the final steps of food preparation. For example, fruit may not be picked and wheat may not be ground for flour. But baking and cooking and other activities necessary for the preparation of an actual meal are permitted. Whatever forms of *melakhah* are permitted on *yom tov* are permitted only to the extent that the results are to be enjoyed during the holiday itself and not afteward. (The case of *yom tov* followed immediately by *Shabbat* will be taken up later, in the discussion of *eruv tavshilin*.)

The limited permissibility of kindling fire on *yom tov* should be noted. Fire may be used for any purpose, including smoking; but whereas a fire already burning may be used to light another and all means of passing the fire are permitted, one may not kindle a completely new fire. Thus the use of matches, lighters, or sparkmakers is forbidden. If fire is to be used during *yom tov*, care must be taken to start one going before the holiday begins. Furthermore, as on *Shabbat*, fire may not be extinguished by any means whatsoever.

Another activity prohibited on *Shabbat* but not on *yom tov* is carrying things from one private domain to another. On *yom tov*, any object that may be handled at all (i.e., anything permitted for use on the festival) may be taken out of doors and into public thoroughfares. Nevertheless, the law prohibiting movement beyond the *Shabbat* boundary still applies.

Similarly, the laws of *muktseh* objects (those forbidden to be handled because their usual use is for forbidden activities) apply on *yom tov* as on *Shabbat*, except that certain kinds of objects may be used, and therefore handled, on *yom tov* that may not on *Shabbat*. Thus, cooking utensils, which may be used on *yom tov*, may also be handled. But one may not handle any other sort of tool, except under the special circumstances that make it permissible on *Shabbat* as well. This prohibition applies to instruments used in delicate work, goods to be offered for sale, raw materials not processed ahead of time to be used on the holiday, and, of course, money.

The festivals, taken as a group, differ from *Shabbat* in their positive content as well as in their restrictions. *Shabbat* is basically a day of respite, a day devoted to the pleasure of living and to the intimacy between the People of Israel and its God. God's love comes to Israel as a gift, and it is this gift that is emphasized in the *Shabbat* liturgy with the repetition of the phrase "in love." For *Shabbat* itself emphasizes the tie of partnership and identification between Israel and the Creator. The festivals, on the other hand, are commemorative in nature, referring back to and celebrating events in the history of the Jewish people. The element of joy, *simhah*, is altogether more prominent in the observance of the *yamim tovim* than in that of *Shabbat*. Thus the term *simhah* is also a key word in the festival prayers and benedictions, and many of the prescribed observances on those days are intended to foster feelings of joy.

In the Torah, the idea of joy and the commandment to rejoice—"You shall be glad on your festival day"—have many facets. When the Temple stood, the three great pilgrimage festivals—*Pesah*, *Shavuot*, and *Sukkot*—were times of rejoicing in Jerusalem. But the imperative to rejoice on these days was not abrogated by the destruction of the Temple and the end of obligatory pilgrimage. As much as possible, we wear festive clothing, even finer than that worn on *Shabbat*, and buy gifts for all the members of the family in honor of *yom tov*. New clothing, jewelry, toys for the children—all are in a sense part of the *yom tov* obligation and are appropriate for every day of the festival. On these days the Jew has a special obligation to gladden the heart of the downcast, particularly the poor, orphans, and widows. One does not make provision only for one's own celebration but helps others to celebrate as well, be it with money or, even better, by inviting them to join those more fortunate at holiday meals.

On the evening of the festival, as on *Shabbat*, candles are lit in honor of the day. Customs vary in this regard. Some women light the candles before sundown, others just before *Kiddush*, this delay being permissible on *yom tov*. There is a special *Kiddish,* concluding with the "*Sheheheyanu*" ("who has kept us in life") benediction, thanking God for having allowed us to reach this joyous occasion.

As on *Shabbat,* there are four services: *ma'ariv* (the evening service), *shaharit* (the morning service), *musaf* (the "additional" service), and *minhah* (the afternoon service). *Hallel,* a group of psalms of praise, is recited following *shaharit* on all festival days, and special selections from the Torah are read. It became customary to abbreviate the festival services to leave more time for simply enjoying the day. At the end of the festival, *Havdalah* is recited, albeit a shortened version, without the benedictions over fire (which has been in use all through the holiday) or spices.

Festivals often fall on *Shabbat,* on Friday, or on Sunday. In each case, certain changes are made in the observance of the day in order to accommodate the special sanctity of *Shabbat.* When the festival falls on *Shabbat* itself, the changes in practice and prayer are slight. The festival *Kiddush* and services are recited, and the special festival Torah portion is read. But in each case, *Shabbat* is also mentioned. And, of course, the sanctity of *Shabbat* is not voided or diminished in the least by the holiday; all the usual prohibitions apply, including those of lighting fire (in any manner), cooking, and baking.

If *yom tov* falls on Sunday, the difference is a relatively technical one: one must make preparations for the holiday (including lighting a fire for the holiday cooking and candle-lighting) before *Shabbat* begins. The evening service at the end of *Shabbat* combines the two observances, for we say *Havdalah* (parting from the Sabbath) as well as *Kiddush* (inaugurating the festival). The two sets of benedictions are said in a complex order, and the texts are more elaborate than usual.

When a festival falls on Friday, there is no change in its observance, but one must take care to perform *eruv tavshilin* ("the mixing of cooked dishes") before the holiday begins. This consists of the preparation of a symbolic dish for use on *Shabbat* that makes it permissible to do other cooking and baking during *yom tov* for the sake of *Shabbat,* if necessary. Other kinds of preparation too—the lighting of the *Shabbat* candles, arranging for food or water to be kept warm over *Shabbat,* etc.— thereby become permissible.

Eruv tavshilin is performed in the following way: holding some bread and a cooked meat or fish dish—or simply a cooked egg—one says the benediction concluding, "who has commanded us to perform *eruv tavshilin.*" Then one says a declaration (in Aramaic, as printed in the *siddur*, or in any other language) that this *eruv tavshilin* is for the purpose of making it permissible to bake, cook, and light fire on *yom tov* for *Shabbat.* Care must be taken not to eat the food during *yom tov*, for then the effect of the *eruv tavshilin* would be cancelled. The law does not require that the food of the *eruv tavshilin* actually be used at any time, but it became a custom to use the bread (usually *hallah*) for one of the *Shabbat* meals, in order for it to find use a second time in the performance of a *mitzvah. Havdalah* is not recited at the end of the festival, because the greater holiness of *Shabbat* has already begun.

Most of the festivals last two days (one in *Eretz Yisrael*), but two of them, *Pesah* and *Sukkot*, are eight days in length (seven in *Eretz Yisrael*). Not all eight days enjoy the full status of *yom tov*, however, only the first two and the last two (in *Eretz Yisrael*, the first day and last day). Since Mishnaic times, the intermediate days have been referred to as *Hol Hamo'ed* ("the secular days of the holiday"). The name conveys the composite character of these days, which are both sacred and profane. The days of *Hol Hamo'ed* are no different from the days of *yom tov* as far as the *mitzvot* of the two festivals are concerned, with one major exception: the prohibitions against *melakhah* do not apply. On the other hand, in establishing the rules governing these intermediate days, the Sages restricted permissible work (*avodah*) to that which must be done to avoid considerable loss. (*Avodah* here refers to a sustained effort such as earning a livelihood, as distinguished from a particular type of physical act, which is implied in *melakhah*.) Gardening, for example, falls under the category of *avodah*, and is forbidden, unless the lives of the plants are at risk.

In practice it is sometimes difficult to know what is permitted and what is not, and customs regarding the observance of these days differ greatly from place to place, from one period of time to another, and from one individual to another. Mourning is not observed during *Hol Hamo'ed*, any more than on *Shabbat* or *yom tov*. The liturgy of these days, like that of *yom tov,* includes *hallel* and *musaf,* but the basic service is a regular weekday one in which mention of the festival is simply inserted in certain benedictions. There is a custom to refrain from writing on *Hol Hamo'ed,* or somehow to do it differently from usual if it must be done at all. (Refraining from writing does not apply to any writing that can cause a loss, whether emotional—such as a misunderstanding or sorrow—or monetary.) Similarly, one avoids getting a hair cut or shaving. (Some modern scholars have permitted shaving, but doubts have been raised about the legitimacy or necessity of this ruling. In general, there has been a trend toward considerable leniency in these matters in recent times, not always well justified in law.)

While all these festivals are prescribed by the Torah as having one day (or one day of *yom tov* at each end of the festival week), the distinction between *Eretz Yisrael* and the Diaspora— one day in *Eretz Yisrael* and two days in the Diaspora—arose in ancient times. There are only two exceptions to this pattern. *Rosh Hashanah* is observed everywhere for two days and *Yom Kippur* for one. The second-day observance is based on the fear that the announcement of the new moon (by which calendar uniformity was maintained in a centralized fashion in ancient times) might be delayed in reaching Jewish communities outside *Eretz Yisrael.* Even after a regular calendar was fixed and published, the Sages insisted that the two-day observance be retained, both out of reverence for time-honored practice and out of concern that it might once again become necessary to rely on natural signs (such as the new moon) to establish dates. Jewish experience in various countries—the Soviet Union among them—shows that this concern is not so far-fetched, that indeed many Jews even today must manage without Hebrew calendars and rely on guesswork as to when the holidays fall.

In contemporary practice there is virtually no difference between the two days of *yom tov.* The exceptions are some minor differences in the hymns and Biblical passages read in synagogue. Also, in extreme situations such as a death on the first day, a distinction may be made, in this case to allow burial on the second day, but halakhically the question is very complex. The institution of the second day of *yom tov* causes certain problems, especially nowadays, for Israelis going abroad and Diaspora Jews visiting Israel. There is an established rule that one's practices should be governed by the place where one makes or intends to make his permanent abode. But there are numerous halakhic issues involved in the question of where a person's permanent abode is—whether it is a matter of intention or of some objective criterion. Until now, scholars and legal authorities have disagreed over the question, and it is best for a traveler to consult a rabbi whose halakhic judgment he relies on, or a local authority, for guidance in each individual case. Sometimes a small change in the situation can affect one's halakhic status in a major way, making it risky to generalize or rely on apparent similarities between one's own situation and that of others.

The day following all three of the pilgrimage festivals, called *isru hag*, serves as a kind of transition in which, according to custom, we bid farewell to the holiday. Thus, *isru hag* still has a bit of festivity about it, halakhically expressed in regard to such matters as mourning and eulogizing the dead and in the elaboration of meals.

═ 18 ═

Pesah

First and foremost, *Pesah* is one of the *shalosh regalim*, the three pilgrimage festivals, and it shares many important laws with the other two. At the same time, the holiday has a distinctive character, revolving around the observances of the seder nights (one night in *Eretz Yisrael*) and the ban on eating *hametz* (leavened food). Indeed, *Pesah* is distinct enough to justify a separate tractate of the Talmud—and a large one at that.

Most of the laws and customs of the seder night are to be found in the standard *Haggadot* and reference works, and so we shall deal mainly with the atmosphere and frame of mind appropriate for that night. The reading and discussion of the *Haggadah* fulfills the obligation to "tell of the Exodus from Egypt," and is in fact the essential observance of the night. But it is not just a night of reading and discussion, nor is the *Haggadah* merely a book of prayers or teachings. The seder is essentially a *rite*. Since we no longer offer up sacrifices, a significant part of the seder ritual amounts to a commemoration of "the night the festival was consecrated" (Isaiah 30:29)—i.e., of the Temple rite of Passover. But the ceremony is also a *reenact-*

ment of the night of the Exodus and of the age-old paschal sacrifice.

Even more than the *Shabbat* meals, the seder is a "family offering," the Jewish family celebration par excellence. The ceremony renews the ties that bind the family together and link it to the past and future. Halakhically it is permissible, indeed obligatory, for a Jew who finds himself alone on *Pesah* to conduct his own seder, wherever he happens to be. But a seder made in fellowship, among people who are akin to one another in spirit or blood, is preferable. In the recitation of the *Haggadah,* in the ritual, and even in the meal (itself an essential part of every festival), a bond is created, not only with the Almighty, but also among those at the table, a "horizontal" as well as a "vertical" connection. The seder night, when mention is made of the blood of the covenant of the first *Pesah* and the covenant of Abraham, is a night when the nation of Israel is renewing its ties with God, as well as the ties among its component parts. The "four sons" of the *Haggadah* often come together around the same table. Their connection to one another and the fact that, despite their differences, they inquire about the same subject, are part of the essence of Jewish unity. Through past and future redemption they are bound to God and hence to one another.

Thus, as long as the possibility exists of experiencing this unit, it is best to join one's family for the seder, even when the family's relationship to Judaism leaves something to be desired. Here, as in many similar situations, the *sharing* of the reading, the discussion, and the meal is of value in itself. While not everyone feels able to take part in communal prayer in the synagogue, the seder offers a much more open, less demanding framework in which to do so. To be sure, not all sedarim are equally beautiful; but as long as even one of the people present really feels the meaning of the occasion, that meaning is conveyed in some degree to the others. Frequently, the seder is led in such a way as to stress ritual details at the expense of the essential meaning of the holiday, or in a way that is overly grim or overly glib. Such one-sided approaches fail to do justice to the *Haggadah* itself, which provides for a rich, varied experience, including solemn rite, lighthearted festivity, intellectual fascination, and familial warmth. Yet even when the right balance is not struck and not all those present are inspired, there remains in every Jewish family a receptivity to the special spirit of this occasion that deserves to be nurtured.

While conducting the seder is largely a subjective matter, involving feelings and attitudes, the other major *Pesah* observance, the ban on *hametz*, is the subject of much halakhic elaboration. The essence of the ban, as it appears in the Torah, is a prohibition against eating or deriving even indirect benefit from the "five cereal grains": wheat, barley, oats, and two grains whose identity is uncertain, *kusemet* and *shifon*. This ban applies throughout the festival. Once these grains have reached a stage of fermentation known as *himutz*, they become strictly forbidden for use on *Pesah*. It is not a simple matter to define *hametz* scientifically, but *halakhah* supplies a number of clear operational definitions. For all practical purposes, it includes most baked goods and dough products, except for dough made under special supervision to avoid fermentation. Once baked, the latter is referred to as *matzah*. Also included are beverages, such as beer and whisky, made from fermented grain.

The prohibition against *hametz* is very severe. Indeed, the punishment for deliberately transgressing it is *karet* (being "cut off" from the Jewish people), the same as is ordained for eating on *Yom Kippur* and other serious transgressions. Unlike other food prohibitions, that against *hametz* applies even to the smallest amounts, the slightest admixtures to permissible foods, and uses other than eating. The secondary laws concerning *hametz* are also quite stringent; even authorities that tend to be lenient in other matters are usually strict in this case. As a result, there is hardly a food that has undergone any kind of processing that is not suspect. (Fresh meat, fish, eggs, and produce are not a problem.) Though there are differences of opinion, it is best to be strict about cosmetics and drugs as well, for here there is a danger of making use of (deriving benefit from) *hametz*.

Some trace of *hametz* may be present in a given product even when its listed ingredients seem perfectly permissible. There are also certain ingredients that may or may not be *hametz*, depending on their origin; alcohol, for example, is permissible as long as it is not made from grain. As a result, it is almost impossible for the layperson to know whether or not a particular product contains *hametz* and it is best to use only those with a bona fide rabbinical *hekhsher* (stamp of approval). The words *kasher lepesah* or the assurances of shopkeepers alone are unfortunately not reliable, and can, intentionally or otherwise, be misleading.

Another kind of difficulty arises from the custom among various groups of Jews of refraining on *Pesah* from using certain plants that the Torah itself permits. Included are rice, corn, and legumes (peas, beans, etc.); the Hebrew word for legumes, *kitniot*, is used for the entire group. All Ashkenazim adhere to this practice, but Sephardim do not. Certain Sephardic groups have taken upon themselves other prohibitions. Added individual and family strictures have also developed, some of them quite strange. There are no clear limits as to how far such prohibitions can be carried. Because of these differences in custom, the label *kasher lepesah* can often be insufficiently specific and thus misleading. For the same reason, it has long been the practice of many pious Jews to avoid eating in other people's homes during *Pesah*.

Here, as in other areas, the beginner would do best to try to observe the essentials and not allow an excess of zeal to lead him to take on too many extra restrictions. These could be difficult for him to adhere to later on and could get him into trouble, practically and spiritually. To mention one common example, most people who follow Hasidic custom do not eat *matzah sheruyah*—i.e., *matzah* that is kosher in every respect but that has been soaked in or has even just come into contact with liquids. This practice severely reduces the range of foods that can be used during *Pesah*.

Cooking and eating utensils used during the rest of the year are as a rule not used during *Pesah* in case they have been used for *hametz*. Such utensils *may* sometimes be used if they have been "kashered" (purged) in a special way (see Chapter 19). The many different ways in which utensils are made and employed makes the question of kashering them complex, so that here too it is advisable to consult someone more expert in such matters. The best solution, to the extent it is feasible, is to buy new sets of dishes, flatware, and cookware to be used only during *Pesah* and put away during the rest of the year. Because the seder table should look festive, it is a tradition to buy especially beautiful utensils *only* for *Pesah* time, then "relegate" them as needed for use at other times, taking care to preserve the separation of meat and dairy utensils. (*Pesah* utensils are kosher for use at any time.)

Not only must dishes, flatware, and cookware used the rest of the year be kashered; so must sinks used for dishwashing and stoves. Indeed, stoves can pose more of a halakhic problem than utensils. In all such matters, *halakhah* should be investigated so as to avoid mistakes based on insufficient information.

The complexity of preparing for *Pesah* means that plenty of time must be allowed if it is to be done correctly and easily. By late morning on the eve of *Pesah*—the exact time varying from year to year and place to place—one is already forbidden to eat or make use of *hametz*.

Though most observant Jewish families make their homes and places of business as free of *hametz* as possible during *Pesah*, it is quite difficult in practice to make them totally so, especially in the case of stores and restaurants, and especially the utensils. For this reason, the Sages instituted the "sale" of *hametz*, a formal agreement in which all *hametz* found on premises owned by a Jew is signed over before *Pesah* to a gentile (who is, of course, not bound by the prohibition); he then "sells them back" when the holiday is over. This transaction is an extremely complicated one, for it must satisfy the requirements both of Jewish law and the law of the land. In most communities the rabbi arranges the sale on everyone else's behalf. Since this cannot be done without the consent of the actual owner, the latter must take the initiative to approach the rabbi (or his deputy) and give him the necessary authorization. (In emergencies, this may be done by phone, and it is better to do it that way than not at all.) *Hametz* and utensils used for *hametz* that have remained in Jewish hands during *Pesah* (*hametz she'avar alav hapesah*) cause many halakhic problems afterward. Thus it is important to arrange the sale in time. One who expects to be away from home on the eve of the holiday can make the necessary arrangements long in advance. In any event, food and utensils to be sold are put away in a special place, so that they are not used by mistake during *Pesah*.

Eating a certain amount of *matzah* on the seder night(s) is a positive *mitzvah* from the Torah itself. For the rest of the holiday it is sufficient to refrain from eating *hametz*. *Matzot* kosher for *Pesah* (not all *matzot* are) are widely available, but there are many special restrictions regarding *matzah* that people take upon themselves. At the very least, one ought to be especially exacting about the three *matzot* used at the seder itself to fulfill the *mitzvah*. Many people "enhance" the observance by using for this purpose only *matzah shemurah—matzah* prepared under particularly careful supervision—or hand-made *matzah*.

The special halakhic regulations of *Pesah*, both the prohibitions and the positive commandments, are all connected with food. This does not mean that food is the exclusive focus of the holiday. Both in terms of its historic origins and purpose, and the emotional overtones that have come to be associated with it over time, *Pesah* has become the feast of the Jewish family, the immediate nuclear family as well as the larger historic and metaphysical family.

Of course, *Pesah* does have a universal human meaning, that of freedom. It is expressed, however, in a very specific way— as the historic liberation of the Jewish people from slavery in Egypt and its formation as a special people. The Exodus from Egypt is an archetype, the model of redemption in general and of the dream of freedom of the people of Israel in particular. In the *Pesah Haggadah*, as in all the texts recited during the holiday prayers, there is an element (appearing overtly and covertly) of messianic hope for a total redemption. More than anything else, *Pesah* is the memorial of Jewish history from its beginning with the Exodus, through the First Temple and the Second Temple periods, to the generations following. This historical and national connection has for the people of Israel a distinct family flavor; the great Jewish family continues to be together in order to refresh its common memories and to strengthen not only the connection with the past, but to reinforce all the present ties binding the family.

The colorful ceremony of the seder was from the start intended to create a memorable impression, to bind childhood memories with the adults and elders of the family, and to unite the past and present. Sharing special rituals and foods brings the whole family together as a distinct entity. Several aspects of the seder are calculated to introduce the active participation of the little children and to leave an emotional imprint. These memories, founded on the combination of all the senses—sight, hearing, taste, touch, and smell—endure long past childhood and fortify the future.

$=$ 19 $=$

Kashrut

Undertaking to observe the Jewish dietary laws, both inside and outside the home, is one of the most important steps the *ba'al teshuvah* can take.

The laws of *kashrut* are distinctive in a number of ways. On the one hand, even for a person who is conscious about food, it is essentially a negative observance: refraining from eating certain things and in certain places. Whatever positive acts are entailed—certain kinds of preparation, for example—have no intrinsic meaning. On the other hand, it is not an observance confined to particular times or places. One must be concerned about it everywhere and at all times. To understand and accept *kashrut*, one must recognize its routine, everyday character. This character reflects, in turn, the character of Judaism itself, which is not just a matter of faith or ritual but of an entire framework and way of life.

Because *kashrut* is an ongoing pattern of life rather than a discrete act, it exerts its influence, in part, indirectly. The Jewish dietary regimen, like all human eating practices, has a significance beyond the act of eating per se.

In the Middle Ages, many scholars, including some of the

greatest, tried to explain the laws of *kashrut* in rational and quasirational ways. These explanations were not very convincing even when they were first propounded; today they often seem far-fetched and irrelevant. It must be remembered that neither in the Torah itself—in Leviticus 11, Deuteronomy 14, nor in any of the other scattered references to the dietary laws— nor in any of the other basic sources of Jewish tradition is there any attempt to justify *kashrut*, except in a general sense, as the way in which Israel's holiness as a people is to be established. To paraphrase these sources, the observance of the dietary laws—eating certain foods, refraining from others—is part of the mystical and biological basis of Jewish existence. It is the "Jewish diet," an integral part of Jewish culture. Of course there are innumerable "explanations," homiletical and mystical, of the various details of the dietary code. But in the final analysis, the code itself is simply a part of the larger legal structure set forth in the Torah as the distinctive framework of Jewish life.

Kashrut also has a social dimension. The fact that the observer can no longer eat wherever he pleases sets up a certain barrier between him and those around him. The positive side of this is that a kosher household is one in which every Jew can eat and feel at home. Thus the observance of *kashrut* marks a meaningful step in defining oneself as a Jew, both in the sense of what one separates oneself from and in the sense of what one joins.

In many cases, taking up *kashrut* also affects significantly one's relations with one's family, for it cannot be observed in the home without the co-operation of all who live there. From now on, the *ba'al teshuvah*'s spouse, parents, siblings, or children must take certain requirements of his into account and, to that extent, change their lives in accordance with his decision. In the best of cases, this leads to a new harmony and sense of Jewishness among the members of the family. In others, conflicts break out.

From a practical point of view, whether or not the would-be *kashrut* observer lives in a major Jewish center, where kosher food is readily available, makes a great difference. If he does not, he may have to make some fairly difficult adjustments.

Like many other areas of *halakhah*, the laws of *kashrut* are quite complex, particularly when it comes to ambiguous cases. But the general pattern is fairly simple. The following is a classification of the kosher and non-kosher foods:

I. Minerals

All materials of inanimate origin are kosher without question, no matter how they are prepared.

II. Produce

A. If grown outside *Eretz Yisrael*, fruits and vegetables are kosher, as long as any cooking is done with kosher utensils and anything added is also kosher.

B. If grown in *Eretz Yisrael*, most types of produce are subject to tithes (*terumot* and *ma'asrot*). Tree fruits are not permissible if picked before the tree's fourth growing season (*orlah*). Problems also arise because of the laws of the sabbatical year (*shemittah*). For these reasons, rabbinical supervision over the whole distribution chain is required, and, in fact, the larger distributors in Israel all have such supervision. Produce bought directly from the grower or in other ways may not have been supervised and is thus problematical. Because these prohibitions do not apply in the Diaspora, many people who come to Israel, including pious Jews, are unaware of them. To eat untithed produce (called *tevel*) is, like all negative *mitzvot* specific to *Eretz Yisrael*, a serious violation.

Unfortunately, it is sometimes impossible, without doing real detective work, to be sure that particular produce offered for sale is kosher. Thus, when buying Israeli produce or any product containing it, the following procedure may be observed to avoid transgression: before eating, and preferably just after buying the food in question, separate a little more than one percent of it and say, *"Hareini mafrish terumot uma'asrot kefi takanat hakhamim"* ("I hereby set aside tithes according to the ruling of the Sages"). The portion set aside should then be burned or thrown away, but not before being wrapped. (This method, which many people observe with all plant products, was devised as a shortcut for those unfamiliar with all the details of the pertinent *halakhah*. The full procedure for setting aside tithes is more complicated, and printed guides are available for those who are interested in following it.)

III. Wine

Grape wine poses a special problem. There is an ancient prohibition, mentioned in the Book of Daniel, against drinking gentile-made wine and even wine in unsealed vessels that have been handled by non-Jews. The prohibition extends to any beverage made from wine or in which wine is an ingredient (brandy, champagne, etc.), as well as to grape juice. There is no restriction against alcoholic drinks not made from grapes, such as whisky, beer, and most liquers. (Such drinks may, however, be unfit for use during *Pesah*; see Chapter 18.) When one has a non-Jewish guest, it is best not to serve wine altogether, to avoid problems of *kashrut* as well as embarrassment.

IV. Baked Goods

All kind of bakery products raise questions about ingredients. Even where local law requires that ingredients be listed on food packages and no forbidden ingredient appears, it cannot be safely assumed that none is present, for things included in very small amounts do not have to be listed. Whether animal fat was used to grease the pans or ovens is also unknown, and can have crucial implications for *kashrut*. Thus one should always look for a *hekhsher* (rabbinical seal of approval) on the package or a *kashrut* certificate in the bakery. An exception is Jewish-baked bread sold in Israel, particularly that produced by the larger bakeries, which are under rabbinical supervision. Such bread may be assumed to be kosher. If there is any question as to whether the grain used was tithed, a piece of the bread (or cake) may be broken off for this purpose, fulfilling at the same time the mitzvah of *hallah* (see the following).

The situation in the Diaspora is more complicated in this regard. As early as Second Temple times, the sages forbade eating "gentile bread" (*pat nokhrim*), but the observance of this rule has had its ups and downs through the ages. Today, in places where extra ingredients are put into bread, such as the milk that is usually added in Holland, the ingredients must be checked for *kashrut*. If Jewish bread (*pat yisrael*) is available, it is to be preferred. If not, other bread may be permissible.

As for home-baked bread and cakes, attention must be paid to the *mitzvah*, commanded in the Torah, of setting aside as a gift for the *kohanim* (priests) a certain amount of every batch of dough. This gift is called *reshit arisoteikhem hallah* ("the first yield of your baking," Numbers 15:20), or simply *hallah*. Since nowadays the *kohanim* cannot prove their lineage, the hallah is not actually given to them, but it must still be set aside in a symbolic way. If the batch of dough in question amounts to at least *omer haman*—thought to be about 1500 grams or 3 pounds 5 ounces—a small piece is broken off and burned, while reciting the benediction ending "who has sanctified us with His commandments and commanded us to set aside the challah." This *mitzvah* applies only to the person who does the actual baking. But for various reasons, some of them esoteric, it is especially praiseworthy for the woman of the house to do it.

To avoid confusion, cakes made with dairy products or pies made with meat should be given distinctive shapes.

V. Animal Products

A. All **invertebrates,** including clams, scallops, snails, oysters, crabs, shrimp, lobsters, and all kinds of insects, are forbidden. This rule has two exceptions. Theoretically it is permissible to eat certain kinds of grasshoppers, something that was in fact done in a few Jewish communities in North Africa and Yemen. Of more immediate relevance, the Torah permits the eating of honey, which, though it is made by bees, does not include any part of their bodies.

B. **Amphibians,** such as frogs and toads, and *reptiles*, such as lizards, snakes, and turtles, are all forbidden.

C. **Fish** that have fins and scales are permitted; other fish are not. This division corresponds roughly to the zoological one between bony and cartilaginous fishes. The presence of readily visible, easily removable scales is a simple, reliable indicator of *kashrut*. Thus shark, eel, and catfish, for example, are forbidden. There are certain fish, such as swordfish, whose halakhic status is unclear, and whether or not they are considered kosher is a matter of local custom. As in the case of other animals, the division between kosher and non-kosher fish also applies to products derived from them, such as fish oil and caviar. Some caviar is kosher, some not.

Once a permissible fish has been caught and killed, by whatever means, there are no halakhic requirements as to whether or how it is to be used. It may be eaten in its entirety, including the blood. (Living flesh—*ever min hahai*—is, of course, strictly forbidden.) While fish is considered neither "meat" nor "milk," there is an ancient custom not to cook or eat it together with meat. Rather, one pauses between fish and meat courses, and may even drink or eat something else at that time. It is also customary not to fill a vessel with fish blood without labeling it as such, to avoid giving the appearance of consuming the blood of mammals.

D. All **other aquatic and marine animals,** including mammals (seal, whale) and their products, are forbidden as food.

E. **Fowl** are divided by the Torah into "clean" and "unclean" species (*tamé vetahor*). Not all the unclean species listed are identifiable to us, although the Sages supply descriptions of them. Thus, in practice, only a few birds are definitely kosher, among them the domestic fowl: chicken, turkey, duck, goose, and pigeon.

Though a given species may be permissible, a particular specimen of that species must qualify in several other ways before it can be eaten. First, it must be slaughtered according to *halakhah*. Any other manner of death renders it *nevelah* ("found dead") and thus forbidden as food. Nowadays, *shehitah* (kosher slaughter) is done by professional *shohtim* (singular: *shohet*), whose practical and theoretical knowledge is rabbinically certified. The *shohet* must also ascertain that the bird was not previously damaged in any serious way by disease or injury, which would make it *trefah* ("torn") and thus unfit to eat.

After proper slaughter (and plucking), a series of procedures must be followed, the purpose of which is to purge the carcass of as much blood as possible. This is called *hakhsharah* ("kashering"). Allowing for some technical complexities and minor local variations, the general procedure is as follows: The heart and major blood vessels are removed and the carcass is soaked in water for 30 to 60 minutes. It is then placed on a perforated tray or pan (of any material) and salted all over using coarse ("kosher") salt. After one hour, the salt and blood are rinsed off thoroughly, and the meat can be cooked and eaten.

Meat that is to be broiled on a perforated pan or spit need not be kashered in the manner described, but is simply salted a little before cooking. If, however, it is to be fried, it must first be kashered. Liver cannot be kashered by soaking and salting but only by broiling, after which it can be cooked in some other way as well. The vessels used to collect the blood during kashering are not usable for any other purpose. Fowl sold in most kosher butcher shops, and frozen kosher fowl, come ready kashered.

F. **Mammals** are divided by the Torah into permitted and forbidden, the permitted mammals being those that both chew the cud and have cloven hooves. Thus, such domestic animals as the cow, sheep, and goat and such wild animals as the deer and its close relatives may be used. (Theoretically, the giraffe and the okapi are also permissible.) All other mammals are forbidden; halakhically there is no difference between the prohibition against horse and camel meat and that against pork.

The rules regarding *shehitah* and *trefah* in the case of fowl apply here as well. An animal that is improperly slaughtered or found to have been previously damaged may not be eaten. Damage is much more common in mammals than in fowl, so a more thorough inspection is made after slaughtering them. Some make a point of eating only *glatt* ("smooth") animals, those in which no imperfection whatsoever turns up, either in the slaughtering or in the subsequent inspection.

Two special prohibitions apply only to mammalian meat: against eating the *helev* (certain abdominal fat) and against eating the femoral vein and sinews found in the animal's hind legs. There are special *menakrim* ("porgers" in English, derived from the Judeo-Spanish) whose job it is to remove these parts from the carcass. Interestingly, the ancient Chinese gave the Jews in their midst the religious designation of "sinew-removers." In some countries it is more economical not to sell the hind quarters as kosher meat at all than to remove the forbidden parts from them before sale.

G. **Meat and milk.** Another important law that applies to both mammals and fowl is the requirement to keep meat and dairy products separate. The Torah forbids only *cooking* meat and milk together; but to avoid confusion and error, it was eventually ordained that two different sets of utensils should be used and that different people should not eat the two kinds of food at the same table. "Meat" includes many foods that merely contain meat by-products, such as various soups and sauces. It is best to regard food cooked in "meat" pots also as "meat." For each of the two kinds of food (meat and milk), separate dishes and flatware as well as pots and pans should be acquired. It is customary in observant Jewish homes to give "meat" and "dairy" utensils distinct markings to avoid mix-ups. It is best to use separate tablecloths as well, and to wash the two sets of utensils separately. Many houses have separate kitchen sinks for this purpose.

Whenever a "dairy" vessel is used for meat, or vice versa, there are grounds for concern that the vessel has been rendered *tref* (unkosher) and thus unfit for use. If one still wishes, to keep and use the vessel, one should consult a rabbi as to whether and how it can be made kosher once again. (See the following.) The rule of separation applies to all utensils except those of glass, where there is no concern that the vessel may pick up the taste of the milk or meat. Thus the same drinking glasses may be used at all meals. It is mainly with metal, wood, and earthenware utensils that special care must be taken: plastic utensils also cause many problems. It is best, then, to maintain two complete sets of utensils, as has been the Jewish custom since time immemorial.

Most foods are in fact neither "meat" nor "dairy" but "neutral" or *pareve*, to use the obscure Ashkenazi term. Any such food may be safely eaten with either meat or dairy products. Eggs and fish are pareve. Foods with several ingredients, such as baked goods, should always be checked for the presence of either meat or dairy products.

Not only may the two kinds of food not be eaten together, but it has been ruled that a certain amount of time—generally six hours—should elapse between a meat meal and a dairy meal. (In some localities a shorter waiting period is customary.) After eating dairy, on the other hand, a much shorter interval, no more than half an hour, is required before eating meat (except after eating hard cheeses, when the interval is longer).

VI. Kashering Utensils

After deciding to observe *kashrut*, one of the first steps one must take is to kasher (make kosher) one's kitchen and utensils. Since utensils that have been used for forbidden foods are themselves forbidden, even if from then on these utensils are used for kosher foods only, they must either be replaced or somehow made kosher. Buying a new set of utensils and junking the old is a simple yet drastic remedy that few people can afford, and it is not really necessary. There *are* ways of making non-kosher utensils kosher.

Kashering must be done even in homes where some aspects of *kashrut*, such as refraining from forbidden meats, may previously have been observed. This is because meat and dairy food may nonetheless have been mingled or the meat not properly prepared. Only in the case of strictly vegetarian households is there no reason to be concerned about utensils.

The laws of kashering are quite complicated, and the complexity is heightened by the many different ways in which food utensils are made. Thus it is best to get help from someone expert in such matters. (Observant people, even scholars, are not necessarily well-versed in this particular body of laws, and situations often arise in which real expertise is called for.) It is nonetheless important to know the general outlines of the laws oneself, to be able to deal with the simpler aspects of the task unaided and to avoid going astray.

Vessels in need of kashering are classified according to the following criteria: (1) what they are made of, (2) how hot they get when in use, and (3) how they are used: whether dry or with liquids; in direct contact with food or with some other vessel intervening; for boiling, frying, roasting, or baking, etc.

One should not rely on memory as to whether or not a particular vessel has ever been used for nonkosher food, because one who is not conscious of such things does not usually register them at the time. In any case, vessels should be taken out of use for hours before kashering begins.

In many respects, the question of heat is a primary one. If a vessel is never used except with food that is cold or at room temperature, it needs no special kashering but only a good washing. For example, bread containers, cake plates, storage cannisters, refrigerator jars, and the refrigerator itself. Exceptions are knives (even bread knives) and vessels used to store liquids (such as wine) over long periods of time. These require kashering, though they may have never been heated.

The general rule is: a utensil is kashered by thoroughly cleaning it, then plunging it into clear water that is as hot as the utensil itself got when it was made *tref*. A large kosher vessel is used to heat the water into which the utensil is plunged. If the utensil can be put into boiling water, it is best to do so. The utensil is left in the water a short time, then removed. It is then kosher. It is important that all food particles have been removed before plunging (called *hag'alah*); thus, utensils constructed in such a way that food particles can get trapped in crevices cannot be kashered.

This method is effective for most metal pots and pans as well as flatware. Utensils used at higher temperatures, such as broiling pans and ovens, are kashered in the same way they are normally used. If possible, broiling pans are put directly into the flame for a little while. Ovens are cleaned well, lit, and left on for a while at the highest possible temperature. They thus become completely kosher.

In many cases, the materials used in the manufacture of a particular vessel make it impossible to kasher. Thus:

1. Simple, unglazed earthen vessels, and most glazed earthen vessels, can be kashered only in rare cases and by an arduous method that is generally not worth the trouble.

2. Wooden vessels are not usually used with heat, but if they have been, they can often be kashered by purging (*hag'alah*) or rinsing.

3. Ordinary glass vessels, because they are very smooth and are not used at high temperatures—even drinking cups do not receive water that is actually boiling—do not require *hag'alah* but only a thorough washing.

4. Pyrex dishes used for cooking are kashered by purging. (Some people are strict about such dishes and do not regard them as capable of being kashered).

5. Enameled metal vessels are customarily kashered by purging.

6. Porcelain-type vessels used only for drinking can be kashered by washing them in hot water.

7. Different views among the authorities and different customs prevail regarding plastic utensils. If they were used only for cold food, they can be kashered by washing. If they were used for cooking, the local rabbi should be consulted.

8. Utensils made of more than one kind of material or in which several pieces are joined together (by glue or screws) require special inspection to determine whether or not they can be kashered, since it may not be possible to clean or purge them thoroughly.

9. Most electrical appliances have to be checked by an expert. They can usually be kashered by heating them to the maximum temperature, either empty or filled with clean water. Appliances that make use of pressure or in which strong spices have been used require special attention. Mixers, for example, always need to be checked, though as a rule they can be taken apart and each part kashered separately.

Various objects used in connection with food also require kashering, though less obviously so. For example, wooden cutting boards need to be thoroughly cleaned and, if possible, purged. Tables should be cleaned well, since food is sometimes spilled on them. Dishwashers need to be cleaned, then heated to the maximum; but it is best to consult an authority about them. Dentures should be thoroughly cleaned and washed in hot water (or purged, if they are made of material that can withstand the heat).

Kitchen counters and sinks present special problems. If the counters are metal or stone, they should be cleaned as thoroughly as possible, then rinsed with boiling water (using a vessel, such as an electric teapot, that keeps the water boiling right up to the moment of pouring). An alternative is to pour a flammable liquid (turpentine or benzine) over them, light it, and let it burn for a short while. Here too it is best to consult someone expert in such matters, and not only regarding the technicali-

ties. The special problem of the sink is solved today in many
religious households by installing two separate sinks, one for
meat, the other for dairy dishes. If this is impractical, the (single) sink should simply be seen as a nonkosher vessel and care
taken not to let a hot dish or pot touch it. This is facilitated
by putting a rack or platform of some kind in the bottom of
the sink.

Once kashered, utensils to be used with dairy food and
those to be used with meat should be kept separate; tags or
symbols can be helpful. Whenever there is a mixup, the status
of the utensils in question must be rechecked, because often
they cannot be used again until they are kashered. In general,
it is not a good idea to use the same serving pieces, or even
tablecloths, for meat and milk.

According to *halakhah*, utensils that have been in the possession of a non-Jew, even if they have never been used, must
be immersed in a *mikvah* (ritual bath) to be usable. Naturally
if they *have* been used, they must undergo thorough kashering
as well. The law of immersion applies to metal and wooden
utensils but not to earthenware or china. The Sages ordained
that glass vessels too require immersion, and it is appropriate
to immerse plastic vessels as well. As a rule, there is a special
section of the *mikvah* set aside for the immersion of utensils.
If the utensil is metal or wood, before it is immersed one says
the benediction ending, "who has sanctified us with His commandments, and commanded us concerning the immersion of
a vessel [or vessels]." In the case of an electrical appliance that
cannot be fully immersed, a rabbi should be consulted; there
are ways to deal with such appliances.

As a rule, kashering an entire kitchen, even one full of
utensils, takes just a few hours if done properly. Nor is it a
particularly complex operation. It must be done, however, if
the laws of kashrut are to be fully observed.

VII. Shopping and Eating Out

Eating in restaurants and buying prepared food in stores
have become integral parts of contemporary life. In both cases,
one who decides to observe the dietary laws is going to have
problems. First, food that has been processed in any way—

cooked, preserved, etc.—is subject to questions of *kashrut*, in some cases because of the ingredients, in others because of the mode of preparation (in nonkosher vessels, or by gentiles). Thus, no prepared or partially prepared food product should be bought and no restaurant patronized that does not bear a *hekhsher*.

In Israel, this is much less of a problem because most restaurants and packaged foods have *hekhsherim*, and because there is less likelihood of food being *tref* to begin with. Though mistakes are occasionally made in preparation or supervision, the Israeli *hekhsherim* are generally reliable, and establishments that receive them can be assumed to maintain the basic conditions of kashrut.

In the United States and other large Diaspora communities, certain organizations concern themselves with certifying the *kashrut* of meats, packaged foods, shops, restaurants, and catering facilities. Packaged foods bear special registered symbols indicating that they are certified kosher by particular organizations, and kosher dining facilities, both in Israel and in the Diaspora, can be expected to display certificates of inspection provided by a rabbi or rabbinical body.

The real difficulty arises for someone who tries to observe *kashrut* in a place where there are few other observant Jews. He will probably have to "import" food from time to time from the nearest Jewish community. Certainly such a person should consult more knowledgeable people about how to proceed and should exercise the greatest caution. But even where kosher facilities are available, scrutiny is appropriate. Is the certificate of *kashrut* displayed by a particular restaurant or hotel up to date? If in doubt, it is best to check. Though many proprietors of such establishments are perfectly reliable, be they themselves observant or not, there are also unscrupulous business people prepared to exploit customers' trust and lead them to transgression.

VIII. Traveling

Several travel guides for the observant traveler are available in English. Such guides usually list not only kosher eating facilities but synagogues and other Jewish institutions as well.

If further information is needed in a particular place, one can always contact a local rabbi (if there is one) for assistance. As a rule, help is extended warmly, and if a stay of any duration is planned, this contact can be of great importance. But what to do if there is no local Jewish community and no help available? Here are a few rules for keeping *kashrut*:

1. Raw fruits and vegetables are always permissible. If Jewish bread is unavailable, any simple bread with no fat or additives may be used.

2. An ancient ruling, going back to Talmudic times, forbids the use of dairy products (except butter) made by non-Jews unless the milking and processing were done under Jewish supervision. The fear is that milk from nonkosher animals may have been mixed in. A leading rabbi of the last generation ruled, however, that where dairies are under government supervision, their products may be used without restriction. Many observant people follow this lenient ruling.

3. Hard-boiled eggs may be eaten anywhere.

4. Hot drinks such as coffee, tea, and cocoa are always permissible if no milk is added.

5. Alcoholic beverages, apart from wine and wine derivatives, are always permissible.

Many people find it practical to eat in strictly vegetarian restaurants. In addition, most airlines and many steamship companies and hospitals will provide kosher meals if they are requested in advance. In short, the observant traveler may have to limit himself, but he can manage.

As we have seen, *kashrut* represents a complex system of rules, both wide and narrow in their scope, which come into play in different ways in different situations. It may be difficult for the beginner, but eventually it becomes a part of his way of life, meaningful and far-reaching in its social consequences, yet no longer problematic.

20

The Home

A truly Jewish home should glow with an inner light. The presence of committed Jews there makes itself felt no matter what the external forms. A home bespeaks the personalities of its inhabitants; a Jewish home radiates Jewishness. Nevertheless, tradition and law require us to display certain distinguishing signs, signs that have not only a personal significance but a commonly understood symbolic meaning and an objective value.

These signs have a number of desirable effects, first and foremost on the inhabitants themselves. The external demands placed on us as we go about our affairs, particularly in the fast-moving, fast-changing world we live in today, make it all the more important for us to maintain and strengthen our inner lives. In everyday life, most people find themselves in a seductive, all-embracing atmosphere that is neutral, at best, toward spiritual values. It is thus important that when we return home we feel, consciously and unconsciously, that we are returning to our true selves. The objects we surround ourselves with have a deep meaning for us, and as we become habituated to them, they establish our sense of home and our sense of ourselves.

Jewish objects help make for a home—and a self—that are in-
wardly as well as outwardly Jewish.

A second consideration involves the people around us,
who relate to us, to some degree, according to the outward signs
we present. When people know that a home is Jewish, they
treat it as such—again, consciously or unconsciously. Some
things are said and done in a Jewish home while some are not.

A third, and extremely important factor is the effect of
Jewish home symbols on the family, and particularly on growing children. As the child absorbs the atmosphere of the home,
he or she also internalizes images of its physical artifacts in a
particularly meaningful and lasting way. Thus, in later memories of childhood, such symbols often play an especially important role, and they can be decisive in the formation of identity. A home that is filled with Jewish symbolism helps instill
Jewish consciousness in a way that one of "neutral" appearance
cannot.

The primary *mitzvah* concerning the home, a *mitzvah* enjoined in the Torah itself, is that of the *mezuzah*, the "trade-
mark" of a Jewish house. The *mezuzah* consists mainly of a piece
of parchment (*klaf*) inscribed with two passages from the Torah,
one beginning with the words "Hear, O Israel" (Deuteronomy
6:4-9) and one beginning with the words "It shall be when you
hearken" (Deuteronomy 11:13-21). These passages set forth
some of the principal elements of the Jewish faith, and both
mention explicitly the *mitzvah* of affixing the *mezuzah*. The in-
scription must be written by a pious scribe; copies made on
paper or printed are not kosher. The *klaf* is protected by inserting it into a special container called a *beit mezuzah* (*mezuzah*
case). There are no halakhic requirements concerning this
container, either as to size or shape, and it has thus taken a
great variety of forms, traditional and innovative, simple and
ornate.

The *mezuzah* is mounted on the doorpost, i.e., the wooden
or metal side-piece of the door frame (this is the literal meaning
of the word *mezuzah*) outside the door, on the right as one enters. Questions as to what constitutes the "right" side or how
to mount *mezuzot* in doorways of unusual construction should
be taken to a scholar. *Mezuzot* are placed in every doorway in
the house except those leading to bathrooms, which it would

not be appropriate to dignify in this way. When affixing the *mezuzah* the following benediction is recited: "Blessed art Thou, O Lord our God, King of the Universe, who has sanctified us by His commandments, and commanded us to affix the *mezuzah*."

The *mitzvah* applies to any household inhabited by a Jew. In *Eretz Yisrael* the obligation must be fulfilled immediately upon taking up residence; elsewhere, within thirty days. The *mitzvah* applies equally to single people and families, men and women. Thus, either husband or wife can affix a *mezuzah* and recite the benediction.

There are various customs as to how the *mezuzah* should be affixed. The Ashkenazic custom is to place it one-third of the way down the doorpost, or, if the doorway is particularly high, not above human height. The *mezuzah* is inclined slightly toward the interior of the house. The Sephardim place it straight up and down, a little more than halfway up the doorpost. It is customary to show reverence for the contents of the *mezuzah*—which include, as we have noted, some of the essential teachings of Judaism—by touching or kissing it whenever one enters or leaves a house.

One does not remove a *mezuzah* on moving out of a house unless the new occupants are non-Jews. Various beliefs have grown up around the *mezuzah* over the centuries, but the essence of the *mitzvah* is the expression of our constant devotion to God, to the extent that we even inscribe the words of His Teaching (Torah) as a reminder on the doorways of our houses. Because the *mezuzah* is the sign par excellence of a Jewish house, its presence is in effect an affirmation of the residents' Jewishness. For this reason, the *mezuzah* is mounted outside the door, where it will be visible to passersby.

While the affixing of the *mezuzah* is a *mitzvah* set forth in the Torah itself, there are other things, too, that give a house a "Jewish appearance." One of the most important is *sifrei kodesh* (Jewish holy books). Some Jewish families for various reasons have actually kept *sifrei Torah* (Torah scrolls) in their homes. Today, books other than the Scriptures are significant as well. The presence of books in the house, and their accessibility, are not just a matter of convenience for reading and study. Their very conspicuousness is a reminder that they *should* be used—at the very least looked into from time to time. Children are tempted to open and delve into them. Books generate a special atmosphere.

According to *halakhah*, *sifrei kodesh* are to be treated reverently, almost in a human fashion, as honored guests in the home. They are not placed anywhere that is unworthy of them; members of the household do not undress or have sex in the same room where such books are kept. Custom has it that they are never placed upside down, while law requires that they are not left open when not in use.

Another custom that lends a Jewish look to a house is that of keeping a *tzedakah* (charity) box on hand. Of course, one cannot discharge the obligation to give *tzedakah* in this way alone. (We will have more to say about the importance of this *mitzvah* in Chapter 24.) But the *tzedakah* box—be it a personal one out of which one gives to the poor, or a box belonging to a social or religious-educational institution—is part of one's ongoing self-education and the education of one's children. It is a constant reminder of a Jew's obligations to society, of the fact that the religious life is not confined to ritual alone but entails responsibility to others.

An ancient practice, deeply grounded in *halakhah* and Kabbalah, enjoins putting money into the *tzedakah* box before praying. Thus, women do so before lighting candles. And just as some people make it a practice to declare before performing a *mitzvah* that they are doing it "in the name of all Israel," it seems fitting to give *tzedakah*, thereby joining oneself to the needs of others, before performing other *mitzvot*.

It is important to remember that the *tzedakah* box is not just a matter for the rich, who have an extra obligation to be mindful of others' distress, but for every Jew. Once, almost every Jewish home had at least one *tzedakah* box, that of the Fund of Rabbi Meir the Miracle Worker, which cared for the poor of *Eretz Yisrael*. This box served as the sacred focus of many homes, even those of the very poor who themselves depended on the support of others. This awareness of Jewish interdependence undoubtedly carries great significance.

A separate *mitzvah* is based on the verse "This is my God, and I will enshrine Him." The Sages interpreted this to mean: Adorn the *mitzvot* which you perform before Him. Thus, it is in itself a *mitzvah* to make all the accessories connected with the *mitzvot* as beautiful as possible. While the great Rabbis in every generation have cautioned our people against excessive self-adornment, they have encouraged the decoration and beautification of ritual objects. The prayerbook, the *Kiddush* cup, the *etrog* (citron) box, the vessels of *Havdalah*—all have inspired artists and artisans. No set form is imposed, nor is there any need to adhere to the aesthetics of earlier generations. One can, of course, retain the traditional forms if so inclined. But throughout Jewish history, our people have usually adhered to certain motifs while modifying the technique and application according to the period and locale. In any case, beautiful ritual objects are part of the making of a Jewish home.

The issue of decoration also has a negative aspect: Just as there are objects and symbols that breathe a Jewish spirit—for example, the ancient symbol of the *mizrah*, a paper or cloth hanging indicating the direction of Jerusalem—there are also objects that negate a Jewish spirit. Symbols or artistic motifs associated with other religions and cultures are probably not permissible in a Jewish home. The owner may not be interested in the meaning of such objects but only in their beauty; nevertheless, when they are prominently displayed they are bound to have an effect, however subtle, on those who see them. There is a place for such things in albums, perhaps, but not on walls or otherwise in permanent view.

There are other visible signs of a Jewish home whose primary purpose is not symbolic, but are functional outgrowths of the Jewish way of life. One is the separation of utensils used for meat and dairy food. The observance of *kashrut* tends to give the kitchen a recognizably Jewish character which, again, conveys a message to all who see it.

The Jewish quality of a home should not be instilled by adhering to a stereotype or standardized image of "the Jewish home." There is absolutely no need for the individual personality and aesthetic tastes of the inhabitants to be swallowed up by copying any model. Nevertheless, the absence of certain items and, even more so, the emphasis on conspicuous Jewish elements serves to create an atmosphere that affects the whole personality of the inhabitant. The picture of a great person or of a holy place are not only emblems one is identified with, but they also focus attention on certain memories and relationships. Those parts of the house set aside for Sabbath meals or for Torah studies become endowed with their own special significance. The entirety of such an approach makes an apartment into a home and even turns the home into something of a spiritual and educational center.

═══ 21 ═══

The Woman's Role

Most of the problems connected with the role of women in Judaism are not peculiar to *ba'alei teshuvah*. These problems arise from a clash of cultures in which most Jews today are involved. In Western culture, which is dominant today in most countries where Jews live, woman's role is defined quite differently than in Judaism. Nonetheless, the problem is sharper for men and women raised in Western culture who seek to move all at once into the Jewish milieu. The problems faced by the *ba'alat* (feminine form of *ba'al*) *teshuvah* are not so much practical as social and attitudinal. Acquiring an inner understanding will be more important for her, and harder, than just taking on the practical do's and don'ts.

It must be stressed repeatedly that the issue is not one of relative "status" in the one system as opposed to the other. Entering the world of Judaism means entering a wholly different culture, with its own independent system of values and world-view. One cannot live within one culture and still judge it by the criteria of another, nor is there any point in doing so. Whatever the conclusions of such judgments may be, they cannot be meaningful as long as they are grounded in an external frame of reference. It is only when one opts for an inherently Jewish scale of values that one really becomes part of Jewish life.

According to the Jewish world-view, human society is composed of distinct groups with specific, assigned functions that govern their relationships to each other. Thus the *kohanim* have a particular role vis à vis the rest of the Jewish people, and men and women have particular roles vis à vis each other. Hierarchies (i.e., status differentiations) do arise in relation to certain tasks, but these rankings are not fixed. Rather, they change according to the task at hand. In any given situation, each group and each individual has a particular role to play, none better or worse than any other. In the same way, all of God's creatures have their distinct qualities, and there is no point in "casting envious glances at [the rest of] Creation." What is essential is to realize one's own potential to the fullest extent possible, rather than to imitate others. As the sages of *Musar* saw it, "Thou shalt not covet" was a matter of inner attitude, a desire to have someone else's qualities and attainments. At whatever level one finds oneself, an awareness of others can and should serve as a goad to achievement and improvement; but it must not be allowed to spawn mere imitation.

This prinicple is reflected in different ways in a number of the *mitzvot* in the Torah, for example in the prohibitions against mingling species and hybridization. To impose on someone a path that is not suited to him is not to improve but to degrade him. True oneness, Judaism teaches, is not achieved by homogenization but only when each component joins the whole with its unique character intact. Relatedness, affection, and love lose all meaning when distinct identities are obliterated. In the case of individuals as well as that of groups, it is the very existence of benignly perceived differences that makes mutual relationships work.

In Judaism, women's role is different from that of men. They have different responsibilities and different privileges. One must first understand and accept this view in its generality before getting down to specifics. The halakhic notion that "women are a people unto themselves" must be taken at face value as an expression of the different roles of the sexes. Thus, one of the first things a Jewish woman—and particularly a *ba'alat teshuvah*, coming from a different cultural milieu—must get used to is that the things men do in the religious sphere, be it in the synagogue or anywhere else, are not all to be imitated. Women should not emulate men in putting on the *tallit* and *tefillin*, nor should they even want to. Only the *kohanim* lift up their hands to bless the people; no one else has this obligation or this privilege. The fact that a particular *mitzvah* is addressed to a particular set of people (individuals, groups, nations) means that those people are in *need* of it to elevate their souls and come closer to the Holy One, blessed be He. By the same token, those not subject to the *mitzvah* are deemed capable of reaching the level of spiritual elevation God expects of them without it.

Once imitation begins, it often leads one to spend time doing things that are none of one's concern and of little use, while at the same time neglecting those that are truly important. This is not to say that one should never take upon oneself obligations that go beyond what one is commanded to do; but such extra commitments should be weighed carefully to see whether they really add something to one's life, really fulfill an inner need, or are merely a matter of whim. Hearing the *shofar* sounded or blessing the *lulav* may be a powerful personal experience, but they are not *mitzvot* that obligate women, and more pressing obligations should not be neglected in order to perform them. On the other hand, *mitzvot* that are obligatory for women, like daily prayer, are just as binding on them as on men. Throughout much of Jewish history, however, most women were not strict about following this rule (even in more orthodox communities). But in our time it is fitting for every woman, no matter how occupied with household affairs she may be, to pray twice a day, or at least recite one entire prayer service in a day.

The overall halakhic rule—although one with a number of exceptions—is that women are exempt from *mitzvot* that must be performed at specific times (*mitzvot shehazman geraman*). We do not have an authoritative explanation for this halakhic rule, but we have been provided with vartious interpretations in the course of time. One focuses on the practical consideration that a woman's activities in the home, and especially in the urgent care of children, may interfere with her ability to perform *mitzvot* that are restricted to specific times. Another interpretation focuses on the spiritual consideration that halakhic regulations bound to time are intended to mark clearly the passage of time. Because the woman's own biological periodicity put her (in premodern society) in more intimate touch with the rhythm of time, she had less need for any special reminder.

In practice, time-bound *mitzvot* are relatively few in number, at least if one considers only those that come up with any frequency. Thus, women need not put on the *tallit* (which is worn only during the day) or *tefillin* (which is not worn on *Shabbat* or festivals), nor must they sit in the *sukkah* during *Sukkot*, nor take up the four species (*etrog* and *lulav*). (In fact, pious women *have* usually observed the latter two *mitzvot*, and, despite differences of opinion on the matter, those who do are permitted to recite the appropriate benedictions as well.) Among the exceptions to the rule are the *mitzvot* of reciting *Kiddush* on *Shabbat*, lighting *Hannukah* candles, hearing the reading of the *Megillah* on *Purim*, and all the *mitzvot* connected with the seder, all of which are incumbent on women as well as men.

If there is any common denominator to these *halakhot*, it would seem to be that women are less obligated in ritual matters, acts that have a fixed form and are repeated at fixed times. At the same time, there is an emphasis in their case on faith, religious fervor, and matters of the spirit as expressed in a more fluid manner, less encumbered by detail.

This approach, which gives women an added measure of freedom, also applies to the obligation to study the Torah. Here, *halakhah* is complex. There is a general rule that women are exempt from *talmud Torah*, but the rule is subject to considerable qualification. While women need not study the more abstract subjects, they do in fact have to learn about the *mitzvot* that apply to them. Since the latter include all the negative *mitzvot* (with a few irrelevant exceptions) and a good many of the positive ones as well (those that are not time-specific, plus others that apply to women for different reasons), in practice Jewish women *are* bound to study almost all areas of *halakhah*: permitted and forbidden things, *Shabbat* and holy days, etc. Also, since men and women alike are bound to observe certain positive *mitzvot* that involve not action but thought—faith in God, the love and fear of God, devotion to God—the philosophical, homiletical, and mystical literature (*Midrash Aggadah, Kabbalah, Musar*, etc.) that expands on these obligations is also incumbent on women to study.

What then are women exempt from studying? The range of talmudic literature that is concerned neither with practical *halakhah* nor with religious faith. Here too the realm in which women are expected to function is more specifically concerned with real life. It should be added that there is nothing to *prevent* women from studying if they so desire. As Maimonides put it, even though the woman is not commanded to study Torah, to the extent that she is inclined to do so she receives a reward. Women are thus treated with a certain measure of flexibility that men do not enjoy.

Another area in which the Jewish world-view plays an important role, over and above particular *halakhot*, is that of women's appearance. The practice of *tsni'ut* (modesty of dress), as a way of protecting sexual morality and thus the sanctity of the family, is incumbent on both men and women. For women, however, this practice has another significance. Contemporary secular culture gives women formal equality in all areas of life. At the same time, it sets them up as sex objects. This is not to say that women in general are actually loose in their behavior, but that, in obvious as well as subtle ways, the culture encourages seductiveness, in dress, speech, and behavior. A woman must be "attractive," according to whatever definition is current. In the Jewish religious community, on the other hand, the practice of *tsni'ut* allows women to take part fully in the life of society as a person, not a sex object. In matters of sex and love, she reserves herself for one man, her own husband, and for one setting, her own family. Similarly, a Jewish man is supposed to reserve himself for one woman.

This approach does not reflect a negative attitude toward sexual relations per se, as some outside observers (and even some misguided insiders) assume. On the contrary, the intimate relationship between men and women is understood in Judaism not only as a means of propagation but as something essential to the partners themselves in achieving personal wholeness. A man without a woman, or a woman without a man, is considered only "half a body" (*pelag guf*). Thus Scripture relates that "God created man in His image, . . . male and female did He create *them*" (Genesis 1:27)—the completeness of man being contingent on male and female joining together. For this very reason, because the bond is essential to man and woman alike, it must be a connection of singular intimacy and privacy.

Tsni'ut does not mean monasticism. It does not require that a woman make herself ugly, nor does it presume lack of beauty to be a virtue. Women sometimes misunderstand the verse "Grace is deceitful and beauty is vain, but a God-fearing woman shall be praised" (Proverbs 31:30) as a manifesto against pleasantness of appearance, or at least against the effort to look good. Beauty and grace are "in vain" in the sense that they are transient things, and there is more to life than the preoccupation with them. But inherently they are not bad. Indeed, Jewish women are praised for their beauty, outer as well as inner; the fact that "the daughters of Israel are fair" is a source of pride to our people. Beauty is a gift of God, and *tsni'ut* should not be understood as a denial of it. Rather it is a way of showing special appreciation for this gift as something precious and delicate that is not to be wasted by being paraded in the public eye.

The idea of *tsni'ut*, whose motto is "the honor of the king's daughter is entirely inward" (Psalms 45:14), goes beyond the question of exposing or wasting the human body. The woman in this context is the *akeret bayit* (homemaker), which in turn means *ikaro shel habayit*, the "mainstay" of the home. As the Sages put it, "A man's home *is* his wife." The roles of men and women are seen as oriented in different directions. The man's role points outward. It includes *mitzvot* whose purpose is to change the external world. The woman's role points inward, largely eschewing visible actions, but affirming the obligations of the soul. The same is true on a social level: the community, the larger social grouping, is the province of the male, while the home and the immediate family are that of the female. This is, of course, only a general picture, and in practice the pattern of roles is often more complicated. What is good for some people is not good for others. On the whole, while family means both man and woman, it is the woman who creates the environment in which family life takes place.

Anyone who assumes that the homemaker's role is limited to cooking and vacuuming (like many activities, these too can assume an inherent importance, even if they are somehow not highly regarded) belittles and distorts that role. The single most fundamental and influential unit of society is the family. Other social entities (the tribe, the nation, etc.) can be constructed on the basis of the family, sometimes without regard to it or even in a deliberate attempt to root it out; but these other groupings are transitory by comparison. Furthermore, as in the human body (or in the state), the components of the family play various roles and are more or less essential, depending on the circumstances. But, just as the heart is the indispensable organ in the functioning of the body, so the homemaker is the vital element in the family.

The homemaker's role in the family is only partly concerned with the practical side of managing the household. More important is the spirit, the character, the content she gives to the family's life. It is she who sets the tone and gives the direction. The members of the family may take different paths when they leave home, but within its confines they have a common way of life, usually determined by the wife and mother. Her influence is felt, not only in the raising of the children, but also in the life of her husband, their father. Though he may be in certain other respects "master of the house," it is still she who is decisive. As the Sages so pithily put it, "everything comes from the woman"—i.e., for good or ill.

When a woman has more time and leisure, she is able to go beyond the limits of the family circle. Because of their more intimate acquaintance with other families, women have always been the central force in communal welfare and social aid, usually in a noninstitutionalized manner. Philanthropically minded women in every age and in every place have been able to find the proper means of offering emotional and financial assistance to those in need. The large family with many mouths to feed, the lonely individual, the sick, and the poor often suffer in isolation because the community is not aware of their plight. There is a large gap between economic and social distress and public knowledge of the situation. Hence the personal interest and the active involvement of an individual woman can be more important than the organized efforts of an institutionalized body.

Too often, problems concerning the education of children, in and out of the family, have been pushed to the periphery of community awareness by other seemingly more urgent problems. Typically, it is women, who are most knowledgeable about the quality and impact of their children's education, who have actively participated in criticizing, shaping, and improving existing institutions and founding new ones. In addition, the social activities of a community—from the restricted gatherings at home to large-scale entertainment or study groups (for men and for women)—often reflect the efforts of women. In all these areas, women have a central role, and they can exert considerable influence, both privately and through community organizing.

Whether or not the influence of women is always obvious, particularly in the public realm, it is decisive even there as the underpinning of everything that goes on. The saying that "the honor of the king's daughter is entirely inward" is an apt description of the woman's deepest role: to be a "king's daughter" by acting in the innermost sphere of life. The spiritual principle, "the more subtle, the more effective" confirms the potential of the Jewish woman especially when she works behind the scenes, nurturing character and caring for the basic things that make life worth living.

═══ 22 ═══

Marital Relations

The laws of *tahorat hamishpahah* ("family purity"), which
govern conjugal relations, present one of the most difficult challenges the married *ba'al teshuvah* is likely to face. It is not an
easy subject to discuss with anyone: intimate, delicate, embarrassing, and complex. It is also the area of observance where
being the one observant person in the family presents the most
problems. *Tahorat hamishpahah* cannot work unless both spouses
are equally committed to it. Even if they are, it is not easy to
maintain.

The underlying principle is a simple one, grounded in severe, explicit prohibitions in the Torah itself, with certain
"hedges" added on by later sages and Jewish women themselves
down through the ages. The principle is that there may be no
sexual contact and, in effect, no physical contact at all, between
husband and wife during her menstrual period (*niddah*) or for
several days thereafter. Only after the wife has ritually purified
herself can she resume sexual relations with her husband.

The laws of *niddah* are mentioned in two different contexts
in the Torah. On the one hand, these laws are part of the large
and highly complicated body of laws of purity (*tum'ah veta-*

horah). Since the destruction of the Temple, laws of purity have steadily shrunk in their applicability. "Impurity" (*tum'ah*) has a very specific meaning in this context. It refers to a state arising from certain kinds of forbidden contact. The sole practical import of being "impure," however, was that one could not enter the Temple or touch anything connected with the Temple ritual. Thus, with the destruction, these laws became only of theoretical interest to most people. The *kohanim* continued to observe the laws. They continued for a time to receive *terumah* as food, and this, being *kodesh* (holy), could not even be touched in a state of impurity. In addition, the defilement caused by contact with the dead continued to be forbidden to them. For several generations after the destruction there were also groups of *haverim* ("comrades") who kept the laws of purity and impurity, but these groups eventually died out. And since there was soon no longer any way to be purified of corpse-defilement—the worst impurity of all—most of the laws of *tum'ah vetahorah* became null and void. From the point of view of *halakhah*, "we are all impure by reason of contact with the dead." The laws of *niddah* represent one of the few vestiges of this institution.

But the question of *niddah* comes up in the Torah also in another context, that of the sexual prohibitions. Like all the prohibitions in this category, the one regarding *niddah* is quite severe, the punishment for violation being *karet* (being "cut off"). This explains the seriousness with which the ban has been regarded down through the ages and the proliferation of secondary ordinances designed to prevent a violation from occurring.

The period during which all physical contact is forbidden includes the days of actual menstrual flow plus the seven days after the flow ceases. For various halakhic reasons, the total period is, in effect, at least twelve days long, but it can extend for another day or two beyond that. Contact is forbidden with all menstruating women, married or not. An ancient "hedge" around the basic prohibition is the practice of refraining from sleeping in the same bed as a menstruating woman. This additional restriction is said to have a basis in the Torah itself and is also hinted at in the Prophets. The result is that observant couples have separate beds during the *niddah* period. In fact, it is advisable during this period to refrain as much as possible from getting close to one's spouse: sitting on the same couch, eating from the same plate, etc.

The evening after the menstrual flow ceases, the woman makes certain that it is over by inserting some cotton into her vagina. This she does each morning and evening for seven consecutive evenings, and if all that time she remains "clean" she may go to the *mikvah* the following evening to immerse and purify herself. *Tevilah* (immersion), the essential act of purification, is mandated in the Torah. Its purpose is not cleanliness but ritual purity. *Tevilah* may be done in the sea or in a spring or river. Where it is not convenient to use a natural body of water, a specially constructed bath (*mikvah*) is maintained. This must be an installation where water can be collected naturally (e.g., from rain) by various means. The laws governing this construction, which seek to reconcile the requirement for "natural" water with the requirements of comfort, warmth, and cleanliness, are among the most complex in *halakhah*.

Tevilah is not done only in relation to *niddah*. It is an essential part of the Jewish rite of purification in general. For example, to this very day converts to Judaism, men and women alike, must undergo it. It is also a widespread custom, with the force of law, to visit the *mikvah* on the eve of *Yom Kippur* and of the festivals. Many Jews, especially those who follow *Hasidic* customs, immerse themselves every day before morning prayers, and some do it several times a day.

The procedure involves, first, thoroughly cleansing oneself (including, washing one's hair), then entering the bath water completely nude, with nothing coming between skin and water. (Under exceptional circumstance a loose garment may be worn.) One must also immerse oneself completely in the water, with no part of the body protruding.

Much has been written in an esoteric vein about the meaning of purification by immersion. The underlying theme is that it represents a symbolic return to the primal state—of the individual, of life, and of the world as a whole. One who immerses himself sinks back into that primordial reality and emerges as a new creature. His previous life is then of no consequence. It is both renewal and rebirth.

Even for people who feel no hesitation about it, or who

grew up among observant Jews and are thus well acquainted with it, the practice of *tahorat hamishpahah* is not easy. The principal difficulty is the necessity of avoiding contact with one's spouse for such a long period of time each month. This is particularly hard when abstinence is something new, or for newlyweds. (During pregnancy, when menstruation ceases, no abstinence is required.) The avoidance of sexual relations and other erotic behavior does not mean a spiritual severance or a weakening of mutual affection and ties of closeness. Although the couple is not allowed to sleep in the same bed, it is still permitted and even desirable for them to live in the same room. During this period, they should not neglect their clothes and appearance. The Sages have taught that such neglect can bring about alienation on other occasions and create difficulties in the couple's relationship.

Moreover, there may sometimes be a special need for one of the married partners to be spiritually closer to the other during this period. Many women suffer during their menstrual period from physical and emotional discomfort and require additional support and closeness. Both men and women can be in a state of tension that expresses itself on a variety of levels, and this has to be taken into account in order to prevent family discord during these days.

Sometimes, the relationship between marriage partners, irrespective of age, is so grounded in sex that it can hide other aspects of the personality that may prove to be just as important to the relationship. Thus, the abstention period can contribute to a deepening and expansion of the connection by providing the opportunity to strengthen the more subtle aspects of the relationship. Both partners can become more aware of the advantages of speaking together, friendship, and nonerotic closeness.

Social complications may arise when other people do not understand and sometimes misinterpret the practice of *tahorat hamishpahah*. One's own children can pose a problem. There is no one way of handling such difficulties; each couple must find its own. The crucial point is that husband and wife view each other in the Jewish way: with respect, as partners in life, and not just as a means of procreation or mere sexual objects. (Not that the erotic element is invalid, but that, from the Jewish point of view, it is not enough.) When the couple's shared life is characterized by such mutual regard, the period of abstinence may cause them a certain amount of tension, but it will not disrupt the fabric of their relationship.

Of course, when only one spouse is prepared to abide by the regimen of *tahorat hamishpahah,* a very serious situation arises. Here it may help to explain to the resistant partner that the severity of the prohibition is one of the most stringent in the Torah (comparable to eating on *Yom Kippur,* for example) and that, like most sexual prohibitions, it applies to both men and women, so they share equally in the guilt if it is violated. More than any other instance of disagreement, this subject can break up a couple. Since sexual relations cannot be maintained at all according to Torah without keeping the rules of family purity, a couple unable to reach an agreement on this matter is unlikely to remain together very long. Furthermore, children born to couples who do not observe this practice, while halakhically unaffected, are considered blemished and thus are stigmatized in the observant community, in some people's eyes severely so. Thus, while the lives of *ba'alei teshuvah* may be riddled with contradictions and inconsistencies, it is important that they come to some resolution in this particular area. If they are serious about living Jewish lives, they accept this commandment with all its challenges.

Widespread ignorance about the practice of *tahorat hamishpahah* results partly from people's embarrassment in talking about it; even in circles where sexual matters are discussed freely, there is a certain block against this subject. Like many other basic prohibitions, that of *niddah* has no rational explanation. Thus "proofs" of its supposed benefits, such as the idea that contact with a menstruating woman is in some way harmful, are completely irrelevant to the observance. Yet the sages of the *Mishnah* did in fact point out one benefit of the practice: the boredom that often results from unlimited, continuous sexual access does not mar traditional Jewish married life. The interruption of marital relations during *niddah* is long enough so that when the partners do come back together there is a freshness, a youthfulness, and a vitality about the encounter. It is as if each time were "the first time" and they were beginning anew.

Certain misconceptions may inspire fear, often amounting to an almost superstitious dread, of going to the *mikvah*. These misconceptions are deliberately and openly propagated by people hostile to the practice. In fact, it is rare today to find a *mikvah* that is anything but pleasant to use. But if a woman feels inhibited, she should go the first few times to a natural body of water (the ocean or a river), where the stereotype of the *mikvah* will not be a factor. Of course, performing *tevilah* in a place that is neither supervised nor especially constructed for the purpose poses a certain risk that it will not be done properly, and it is important to check the laws and get advice from a knowledgeable person before proceeding.

What has been said so far applies to the usual cases, where there are no special halakhic complications due to irregularities in the woman's period. Where the timing or length of the period varies—sometimes it may last so long that ovulation, and thus conception, are interfered with—special provisions in *halakhah* (and special medical procedures) are followed. But each case must be considered individually.

The *tum'ah* of *niddah* (menstrual impurity) is analogous to the *tum'ah* associated with childbirth, as described in some detail in the Torah. In both cases there is a connection between the question of purity and impurity on the one hand and conjugal relations on the other. In the case of childbirth, too, the *halakhah* requires refraining from sex for seven days after bleeding ceases. In some Jewish communities the practice is to refrain even longer. Separation during this period may be an emotional strain, but it can also be helpful in giving both parents a sense of sharing in the trauma of childbearing. The same restriction applies also after abortion or miscarriage. Instances of unexpected or minor bleeding should be taken up with a rabbinic scholar who specializes in them. Such a person customarily treats these matters with great delicacy, so that there need be no fear of unpleasantness, whether it is the woman herself or her husband who goes to see him.

One might imagine that there would be something repellent about husband and wife sharing "gynecological details" with one another, that the discussion might entail an invasion of privacy. When done reverently, however, it can actually foster a sense of both intimacy and exaltation.

The question of birth control is relevant here. The essence of the relationship between men and women is less a matter of *halakhah* than of *musar* (ethical wisdom) and a way of life grounded in holiness. Nevertheless, the practice of birth control can pose halakhic problems—for example, in relation to the *mitzvah* of *p'ryah u'reviyah* (procreation)—that require knowledge and, in some cases, scholarly advice. Halakhic thinking is not rigidly mechanical, and there is always room to consider individual factors (medical, emotional, economic) in the life of a given couple along with the fixed requirements of the law. One practice that is clearly forbidden is the use of birth-control methods that physically obstruct the flow of sperm into the womb. Other practices, however, such as the pill and the various intrauterine devices, do not fall into this category, so that possibilities of meeting special needs do exist.

The precepts concerning sexual purity constitute the main halakhic framework for the life of the family, but they alone do not define the positive essence of the marriage relationship. The basic philosophical justification for marriage is that it is not only a means for "multiplying," but an intrinsic part of being human. A man or a woman alone is only "half a body"; in the archetype of Adam and Eve, the two are seen as the two parts of a single unity that must return and unite again in the form of man and woman in order to create the whole human being. This mutual complementarity varies from couple to couple. Nevertheless, several ingredients are necessary for a successful marriage: an attitude of mutual respect, loyalty, and sharing of basic values. Passionate love, physical attraction, or mutual intellectual stimulation may be valuable additions, but they are not decisive factors.

The attitude to sex is derived from such an approach. Judaism does not view sex as unclean, as a necessary humiliation for the purposes of increase. Sexual life is seen rather as a physical expression of the union between man and woman, as an act of positive significance in itself, and, at the highest level, as a sacrament. Therefore, even when sexual relations do not lead to birth (when the woman is already pregnant or when, because of age or other reasons, pregnancy is ruled out) it is still considered a *mitzvah*.

Modesty is not the result of shame concerning sex, but of

great respect toward something extremely personal, intimate, and deserving of the greatest sensitivity. Jewish writings throughout the ages have included general guidance and recommended ways of experiencing sex, but very little in terms of absolute prescriptions that could be considered obligatory. Mutual agreement concerning the rhythm and form of sexual relations is one of the few standard elements in the literature, as is the need to be considerate of the needs and desires of the woman, even more so than the man. In these areas, which are not usually dealt with in any frank and detailed manner, *ba'alei teshuvah* should be careful not to undertake too high a standard and try to do more than they can. Such efforts, when people are not sufficiently prepared for them, can cause unnecessary difficulties and crises. Domestic peace is so important that a person may be allowed to act with great flexibility in order to maintain it, renouncing his own wishes and welcoming the desires of the spouse. This domain of family life, so concealed and so complex, demands much more than any other aspect of marriage. One must remember that the two people (even if there is great intimacy between them) are still two different and separate entities, each with his or her own qualities, desires, and weaknesses, each with his or her rhythm and orientation.

23

Dress

Sooner or later the *ba'al teshuvah* must reckon with law and custom concerning the garb appropriate for an observant Jew. Being something highly visible to others, it is a difficult issue to avoid. One's way of dressing amounts to a public statement. Yet there is often a discrepancy between that "statement" and one's true convictions. For example, a person may become highly observant and even go beyond the letter of the law in his practice, yet remain reluctant to give outward expression to that commitment in his mode of dress. Such expression may have to come gradually, as the *ba'al teshuvah* becomes more at ease with his commitment and its consequences for his relations with others.

For men, the primary question is whether or not to cover the head. This practice has evolved from a *minhag* (custom) of the very pious to an accepted norm, incumbent on all observant males. Talmudic law does not require covering the head, though there are hints there that doing so is to be regarded as a sign of reverence. But the practice became more and more widespread, until by the Middle Ages Jewish legal authorities everywhere were unanimous that sacred words (prayers, words

of Torah) could not be spoken, nor sacred precincts (synagogues, houses of study, even cemeteries) entered bareheaded.
Today, too, there is complete halakhic agreement on this question.

Covering the head at all times is a different matter. In Europe it was the universal custom among Orthodox Jews, except
for some in Germany, to do so indoors and out. The most orthodox even did it while sleeping. In the Near East there was
greater latitude in the matter, and many religious Jews only
covered their heads for sacred activities. Keeping the head covered at all times has a kabbalistic significance, leading some to
cover their heads twice—a hat over a *kippah* (skullcap), or a
tallit over a *kippah*—while praying. For various historical reasons, chiefly because most Jews no longer wear a distinctly Jewish garb, the head covering has, for many, taken on the significance of a badge. Once such a view takes hold, it acquires
a certain significance in the eyes of *halakhah*. Even practices
with no inherent meaning sometimes acquire real importance
from the way they are viewed in the popular mind, due to the
notion of *kiddush hashem* (glorifying God) and *hillul hashem* (sacrilege). When a given act comes to be perceived by most people
as one of *hillul hashem*, *ipso facto*, it is so, even though intrinsically there may be nothing wrong with it.

It is for these reasons that covering the head has become
significant and valuable, not because it has any inherent meaning but rather as a conventional sign of belonging to a certain
group of people and of commitment to a certain way of life.
The *ba'al teshuvah* must be aware of this symbolism. On the
one hand, if he does not cover his head, he will be regarded
by the Orthodox (particularly in Israel) as a deviant from the
true path, no matter how observant he is. On the other hand,
if he is not fully observant, at least in public, the fact that he
covers his head may lead others to see him as hypocritical. Indeed, it may cast a shadow of hypocrisy over the entire observant community. Thus, covering the head is an act fraught with
significance that must be weighed very seriously. But if one does
intend to live an observant life, not in secret, as a kind of Marrano, but openly, he should not "separate himself from the
community" but let other people know his intentions in this

symbolic way. By doing so, he actually helps them relate to him and avoids awkwardness both for himself and for others.

Because the male headcovering is not explicitly a matter of *mitzvah,* either in the Torah or in the Talmud, there are no requirements as to how it should be made. Presumably it should cover most of the head, but as to the shape or the materials to be used, there are no limitations. The various types of headgear commonly seen are simply a matter of local or communal custom. Here too, halakhically meaningless details can take on a certain significance in the public mind, so that various kinds of *kippot* may signify very specific things to both religious and non-religious people. Thus, to avoid confusing or misleading people, it is best to find out what the various current significations are.

Another traditional item of male garb is the *tallit katan* ("small *tallit*"). In ancient times the *tallit* (prayer cloak) was a regular part of Jewish men's daily clothing, and of course it would be fringed in compliance with the Torah injunction. But in the Middle Ages, when styles changed and the *tallit* became a ritual article, to be worn only during prayer, the custom arose of wearing a special undergarment whose sole purpose was to fulfill the *mitzvah* of *tsitsit* (the fringe or tassel). Halakhically, this practice is only a custom and not a law, since the obligation of *tsitsit* applies only if one happens to be wearing a certain kind of garment and does not require the wearing of either the garment or the *tsitsit* itself. Nevertheless, the custom took hold, and is today observed in most Jewish communities—again, an instance of a practice introduced by the very pious that became common to all.

The *tallit katan* is generally made in a fairly standard form: an elongated strip of cloth with an opening in the center for the head, and tassels on the four corners. In most communities it is customary for boys as well as men to wear them, and for them the garments are made smaller. But there is a minimum size—about 50 by 150 centimeters— for the performance of the *mitzvah.* There are various views as to the appropriate cut and the materials to be used. The most stringent insist on pure wool, but most religious-goods shops carry a selection of different fabrics. The usual custom is to wear the *tallit katan* under the clothing but to let the tsitsit protrude. However, the rabbis permit concealing the tsitsit whenever it is likely to cause embarrassment or awkwardness. Many also keep it hidden for kabbalistic reasons.

While there are no absolute requirements concerning male apparel in general, certain norms are widely observed. Excessive exposure of the body, especially while in the synagogue or other holy places, is considered immodest and indecorous. In the synagogue, or at prayer anywhere, even if it be only the grace after meals, the halakhah is that one should not dress in a way that would be inappropriate in the presence of an important personage (a prince, a minister of state). This rule is not inflexible, however, and its application depends on circumstances.

The situation is not very different in the case of women. Here too, there is a general requirement of modesty of dress (tsni'ut) and a specific one concerning covering the head. The general requirement is much more stringent for women, however. While halakhah itself does not define modest dress in absolute terms but allows for differences in practice from place to place and time to time, it nonetheless posits certain basic principles that are generally observed. The violation of these principles can pose practical problems for others, since it is forbidden to speak of sacred things in the presence of "nudity."

There is general agreement, first, that a woman's torso should be covered in such a way that it is not visible. There are different customs regarding her limbs. Her upper arms should be covered down to the elbows—even further according to some views—and her legs down to the knees. The law seems to require stockings, though some authorities take a lenient view on this question. Generally speaking, clothing considered provocative or outrageous in a particular context is ruled out. Again, it is not intended that a woman appear unattractive, but that, while looking becoming, she dress respectably within certain bounds.

Slacks present a special problem. Halakhically, what is involved is not just the question of tsni'ut but also another principle, explicitly stated in the Torah, that women should not wear men's clothing (and vice versa). There are exceptions: dressing up on Purim, for the sake of the festivity of the day, or wearing an item of clothing for a practical purpose (e.g., protection against sun or rain) rather than for adornment. From this point of view, whether or not a woman should wear slacks or jeans depends on a variety of factors that are not inherently halakhic. Thus there is no harm in slacks that are made especially for women and are not immodestly cut. In fact, in certain circumstances (on hikes, for example) pants may be *more* modest than skirts. Still, there are communities where slacks are never considered appropriately modest apparel for women. In other communities, it is customary for women to wear pants with skirts over them. (Such was the case in Yemen, for example, for many centuries.) In general, though, whenever a woman appears in mixed company where different customs are observed, she should take into account the fact that the wearing of slacks is not acceptable to all, even though *halakhah* does not absolutely forbid it.

The prohibition that states that "a man may not wear a woman's clothing" (Deuteronomy 22:5) applies also to smaller articles of clothing and accessories—again, depending on local custom. In most places, the use of makeup and haircoloring is considered inappropriate for men and is thus forbidden. In many communities, too, men who shaved were careful to leave a partial beard or mustache for the same reason.

Married women are required to cover their hair. This is an ancient law, already hinted at in the Torah, that has been observed among Jews all through the ages. In some communities, even unmarried women have been known to keep their hair covered, though this custom never became widespread. The law is not related to that requiring men to cover their heads, and it is more stringent. The fact that a married woman covers her hair whenever she leaves the house is a sign of her special status.

The form in which this practice is observed varies from one community to another. In the communities that were under kabbalistic influence—in parts of eastern Europe and the Arab world, and among the Sephardim—the practice was observed more strictly, such that the hair would be covered completely, with none at all showing, not only in the street but at home as well. In some countries, pious women go so far as to braid their hair in addition to covering it. But in most areas of

Eastern Europe and the Middle East it was considered sufficient to cover the greater part of the hair, and this in fact is all that *halakhah* requires. In any case, there is no doubt that *some* covering of the hair, however symbolic, is called for.

In recent times it has become customary in most communities for women to cover their hair with wigs, and this can indeed be seen as fulfilling the requirements of *halakhah*. Married women are not, after all, expected to make themselves "ugly." Nevertheless, there have been scholars who have ruled that wigs too must be covered, particularly when they look so natural that they cannot be recognized as head coverings and the women who wear them are not recognizable as married. But this too is a matter of custom and not of definitive *halakhah*.

In Jewish tradition, and even in very old linguistic usage, "an uncovered head" means unbridled license. By the same token, covering the head, be it for prayer and study, or at any other time, represents, by general usage at least, the acceptance of Divine sovereignty, of the "yoke of the kingdom of heaven."

Another aspect of Jewish dress is the costume for special occasions. Since the synagogue is called a "bit of the holy temple," and one who stands up in prayer is considered like someone who comes before a great king, this may be expressed not only in appropriate behavior but also by appropriate dress. Even though there are no clearly defined guidelines for this, certain customs prevail. The general rule is that a person comes to the synagogue dressed as though going to meet the most important personage in the land. The appropriate dress is thus an essential part of the "royal splendor" intrinsic to prayer and a place of sanctity.

Accordingly, it is a *mitzvah* to honor the Sabbath and the holidays by dressing up for them. Festive dress on festival days is not only an additional expression of the special feeling of these days, but an obligation. Even someone who finds it hard to make ends meet must at least change his clothes in honor of the Sabbath and festivals. It is also traditional for the holiday garments to be more beautiful than ordinary Sabbath clothes. In accord with this tradition, one of the special holiday *mitzvot* enjoins a husband to present his wife with a new dress or ornament in honor of every festival, as part of fulfilling the *mitz-vah* "to be joyous in the holiday."

Of course, clothes do not make the man, and the inner life is more important than its external expressions. Nevertheless, in addition to their part in a person's public presentation, the clothes a person wears influence him even when he is alone. Religious clothing, in particular, serves to remind him that he is never alone because God is with him.

24

Money

Most religious obligations involve bodily actions that one must or must not perform oneself. But there are also certain *mitzvot* that involve a financial investment in addition to a physical act. The *mitzvot* of *tsitsit*, *tefillin*, *mezuzah*, *talmud Torah*, *lulav*, and *etrog*, among others, cost money, sometimes a good deal of money. And there are more or less elaborate— which often means more or less expensive—ways of carrying out such *mitzvot*.

There are two kinds of embellishment in the performance of *mitzvot*, over and above the minimal requirements of *halakhah*. In one, the concern is with the *intrinsic quality* of the artifacts acquired for the purpose of a particular *mitzvah*. This is called *hiddur mitzvah* ("the glorification of the *mitzvah*"). The extra measure of quality may or not be visible to the casual observer. An especially fine pair of *tefillin*, for example, is not necessarily distinguished by its beauty but rather by the extra care taken in writing the scrolls, the high quality of the parchment, or other far-from-obvious details. Some scribes are not only more exacting than others in fulfilling the basic legal requirements, but are also known for their high degree of *kavan-*

166

nah (religious concentration, purposiveness); this too enhances the desirability of their work. But the more desirable, the more expensive (and sometimes, the harder to obtain). An added measure of care may be shown not only in the choice of appurtenances but also in the *manner* in which one performs a *mitzvah*, the degree of exactitude beyond the minimum requirements of the law.

Hiddur mitzvah entails knowing the finer points of the execution of ritual articles, in order to be able to distinguish real differences in quality from mere local variations or superficial peculiarities. All too often, people make the mistake of fussing over details that are not at all essential to the performance of a given *mitzvah,* or even of insisting on features that make a given item less rather than more desirable.

The notion of *hiddur mitzvah* applies not only to ritual articles but also to such things as food. For example, meat that fulfills the normal requirements of *kashrut* may be refused in favor of *glatt* ("smooth") kosher meat, where the animal was in such perfect condition that there was no need for Rabbinic ruling as to whether or not it was kosher. Or *hiddur* may entail insisting on an extra measure of care in the supervision of *kashrut*, different degrees of scrupulousness being possible.

The Sages have ruled that up to one third more may be spent on *hiddur mitzvah,* over and above the usual cost. Some go beyond this, while others do not go this far. Surely one should be willing to spend at least as much for extra quality in religious acquisitions as one is accustomed to doing in other kinds of purchases. Still, certain precautions should be taken. First, one should avoid undertaking a particular *hiddur mitzvah* that is disproportionate to the overall level of observance one has attained. This is even more important concerning the overscrupulous *performance* of *mitzvot* than the overzealous acquisition of ritual objects, which is, after all, relatively harmless. Second, one should not spend so much as to lead to friction or hardship in one's family. In that case, the added merit of *hiddur mitzvah* is far outweighed by the transgression of causing unhappiness, anger, and dissension. Third, one should consider whether extreme zeal in the performance of a certain *mitzvah* is something that can be sustained over time and whether it is proportional to the importance of that *mitzvah* vis-à-vis all the others. Sometimes a person who becomes so fastidious about certain minor details neglects responsibilities of much greater importance. Such disproportion is worse than ridiculous; it can be a serious distortion of one's spiritual life.

Another way of embellishing the performance of *mitzvot* involves the outward, esthetic dimension, seeing to it that the ritual articles and appurtenances one uses are as beautiful as possible in their design and construction. This is called *noi mitzvah*. It too provides a way of expressing religious devotion, but in accordance with personal taste. The normal desire to make one's home and its contents attractive is here applied to sacred purposes, highlighting the religious element in the home and the awareness of its inhabitants. *Noi mitzvah* applies also to clothing worn on holy days. It is not as important as *hiddur mitzvah*, and outward appearance should not be emphasized at the expense of inner quality, either in terms of material outlay or of attention. Certain very beautiful and expensive ritual objects may not, in fact, even be kosher. For example, there are *Hannukah* menorahs that may be very beautiful but are not kosher or suitable for use because their branches go around in a circle, or do not rise up to an even height. In the same way, a wonderfully decorated *tallit* may be disqualified because it is not big enough.

Money must also be spent on books, more specifically *sifrei kodesh*. Everyone should have such books to study, according to his level and interests. Of course one does not discharge one's obligation just by buying books, and once acquired they must be treated with respect (laying them down properly, not dropping them, kissing them when they fall, avoiding certain kinds of activities in their presence). But their very presence in the home, even when not in use, adds something to its character and, directly or indirectly, to the lives of its inhabitants. Moreover, if a book is at hand, there is a chance one may pick it up from time to time and learn something from it.

Aside from the things an observant Jew needs to buy for his own use, there are a number of other *mitzvot* concerning the use one makes of money, some of which have to do with *tzedakah* (charity) and *gemilut hasadim* ("acts of kindness"), or with support for the study and teaching of Torah. The Sages established an upper limit to what one may give to *tzedakah* and to support the performance of *mitzvot*: one fifth of one's income. Still, there have been many authorities who interpreted this limit leniently and who themselves gave more. The norm is for the Jew to give one tenth of his income. There is disagreement as to how the tithe should be calculated—i.e., how income should be reckoned—but there is unanimity as to the obligation, and customarily gross income is taken as the base.

Nowadays it is often assumed that the welfare state takes care of the needs of the poor. While this is true to some extent, there are many kinds of needs, including urgent ones, for which there is no provision in the public welfare structure and which can only be met privately. One of the reasons for this is the highly centralized, essentially bureaucratic character of the modern state, with its rigid categories and definitions that ride roughshod over the peculiarities of individual human situations. What is more, some people are either unable or unwilling to avail themselves of institutional help. At the same time, help from private sources is much less readily available today than it was in the past. In modern urban society, people are strangers to one another; the individual and the family are more isolated than they have ever been. Rarely does it occur to people that their nearest neighbors may be in need, and even if it does, they cannot be counted on to extend help. For all these reasons it is often important to *seek out* the needy.

It is also important to consider carefully *how* the needy are to be helped. Over and above the basic obligation to give, there is the even more important *mitzvah* of helping in the proper way. In some cases, simply giving money is not enough, because the recipient does not know or does not want to know how to make proper use of it. He may waste it on luxuries, while at home there is not enough to eat; or he may spend it harmfully, on gambling, drink, or drugs. Thus, when giving money, it is important to see that it is put to the use intended. Furthermore, people differ greatly in their needs, both quantitatively and qualitatively. Thus we are told that the greatest Sages would give certain people things they lacked but that might seem to us luxuries, because the things were an indispensable part of those people's lives. Attention to the unique problems of individuals has always been an important part of the Jewish way of life. Of course, not everyone is in a position to perform the *mitzvah* of *tzedakah* (called simply "the *mitzvah*" in the Jerusa-lem Talmud) directly on his own. In that case it is important that he give to proper charity collectors, people devoted to the cause who can be counted on to reach out, investigate, and follow through on his behalf.

The "pursuit of justice and kindness" is no less important for the giver than for the recipient. Indifference to the suffering of others is a kind of wickedness, which can be overcome in part by learning to open one's heart to those in need. Acquiring the capacity to see "the other" not as a stranger but as a brother is one of the ways in which the soul is perfected. Thus the Sages tell us that the way to the love of God is through the love of Israel. Selfishness and self-centeredness impede a person in every aspect of his spiritual development. Only by breaking out of this confinement, by learning to see beyond oneself, can one come to see the Infinite.

The *mitzvah* of *gemilut hasadim* can be performed in many ways and on many levels. Maimonides enumerates eight levels in the giving of *tzedakah*, from economic aid that helps to re-habilitate a person and put him back on his own feet, as the highest level, to simple handouts to beggars At each level, per-sonal involvement, good will, and humaneness are no less im-portant than the giving itself. It has been said that the smile of the giver is worth as much as the gift.

In contrast to *tzedakah*, which involves only the giving of money, *gemilut hasadim* may also involve active help on the part of the giver. Such help can take many forms: giving loans or guarantees (which even people who are not poor may need ur-gently at particular junctures in their lives), visiting the sick, burying the dead, helping a person find the means or the proper partner for marriage, attending others' joyous occasions, heal-ing rifts, etc. All these are integral parts of the fabric of Jewish life, and the degree to which one does them says much about what kind of Jew one is. Devotion to God cannot be complete or valid without caring about toward one's fellow human beings. A "God-fearing" person who behaves immorally toward others is in fact a blasphemer; but more than this, he exposes his own piety as hollow and false.

Here too, it is not always possible for a person himself to extend to help required. He must, however, at least try to be helpful in an indirect way, through the agency of those to whose charitable work he gives financial support. Great importance is attached in our tradition to acts of generosity, however small, and this value is continually reaffirmed in symbolic gestures. Thus it is a custom to give *tzedakah* before prayer as a sign of willingness to share the burdens of the House of Israel and support others in need. As a matter of law, one may not refuse a person who asks for *tzedakah* but must rather give him whatever one can, however little that may be. Beggars may not be a pleasant sight, and sometimes they are actually less needy than people who keep their wants out of the public eye. Nevertheless, "thou shalt not close thine hand from thy needy brother" (Deuteronomy 15:7). It is better to err by giving too much than not to give at all. However, as much as possible, one should try to allocate one's generosity to where it will do the most good.

Another kind of giving involves support for the teaching and study of Torah. Many institutions engaged in such work depend entirely on private philanthropy for their existence. In most of them, the students—be they youngsters or adults—are provided with all their needs, on the assumption that serious study is not possible unless basic needs are taken care of. For the giver, such philanthropy also provides an opportunity to take part vicariously in the performance of a *mitzvah* he cannot devote all his time to.

Indeed, the *Musar* literature often speaks of the giving of *tzedakah* in all its forms as an act that is particularly important for the *ba'al teshuvah*, because of its potential as a corrective measure. There are certain mystical aspects to this truth, but on a less-than-mystical plane it means that supporting the performance of *mitzvot* by others can help to compensate for all the opportunities to perform them that one has missed in a lifetime of non-observance, compensate in a way one could never hope to find time to do on one's own. Furthermore, breaking out of the calculus of the self as the be-all and end-all of existence, joining the "I" to the "we," is itself a form of *teshuvah*, a corrective.

The use of money for charity or other *mitzvot* solves a more general problem: the relation to money in general. There have been many approaches to this in Jewish tradition. Some considered money only as a necessary evil and spoke much in praise of poverty. (There were *Tzadikim* who never had any money left in their house because they immediately gave it away to others.) Even those who believed that there was nothing intrinsically bad about wealth and comfort felt strongly that money was only a kind of deposit, a trust or a pledge. Like the gifts of life, health, children or any other gift given to human beings, the gift of money is something a person has to account for: how and for what the gift has been used.

The accumulation of money for its own sake has always been considered a form of idolatry, a worship of Mammon. The lust for money is considered a very dangerous passion that has no self-imposed limits. Whoever is caught up in it can no longer see anything else in the world, certainly not his fellow human beings. The halakhic regulations dealing with money matters are more numerous and more complex than those dealing with many other matters, even those considered central tenets of Judaism. Just as there are obligations concerning kosher food, so there are even greater obligations concerning kosher money. The prohibitions in this area involving the possibilities of theft, fraud, and deceit of all kinds are far more stringent than the prohibitions concerning transgressions between human beings and God. A person can repent for transgressions against God at all times but cannot atone for transgressions against human beings (even on *Yom Kippur*) unless his contrition is expressed by restoring that which was taken unlawfully and by making proper amends directly to those he has harmed in any way.

Even money that is obtained properly and a life of ease that is not derived from the exploitation of others pose risks and problems. Not only is it forbidden for money to be an end in itself, but even when it is a means to something worthy, there is always the question as to whether it is being properly used, and to whose advantage. Setting aside a substantial portion of one's income for that which is holy—*mitzvot* and help to others—can serve to justify the trust of money a person has been given, and may even help him to use the rest of his money and the power derived from it in a proper way.

Glossary

am ha-aretz (pl. *amei ha-aretz*): ignoramus, especially one who does not know Torah

Ashkenazi (pl. *Ashkenazim*): a Jew of northern and eastern European extraction; of or pertaining to the culture of the northern and eastern European Jews

ba'al teshuvah (pl. *ba'alei teshuvah*; f. *ba'alat teshuvah, ba'alot teshuvah*): one who becomes religiously observant

beit midrash (pl. *batei midrash*; Yiddish: *beis medresh*): house of study

Eretz Yisrael: the Land of Israel, Palestine

gemilut hasadim: an act or acts of kindness

hag'alah: the purging of vessels in boiling water

Haggadah: the liturgy read at the family table on the first night(s) of *Pesah*

halakhah (pl. *halakhot*): the body of Jewish law; a particular law

hametz: (lit. "leaven") food forbidden during *Pesah*

hannukiah: the nine-branched candelabrum used during *Hannukah*

hashash: suspicion or grounds for concern, especially in regard to a potential violation of *halakhah*

Havdalah: the ceremony ending the Sabbath

hekhsher: a certificate or stamp attesting to usability, especially of an item of food or a food-service establishment

hiddur mitzvah: extra care or expenditure in the performance of a *mitzvah*, especially as regards the quality of the objects employed

hillul hashem: (lit. "profanation of the Name") sacrilege

173

hillul Shabbat: desecration of the Sabbath

Humash: the Pentateuch

kashrut: the Jewish dietary laws

kavannah: intent, especially in regard to a religious act

Kiddush: (lit. "sanctification") a benediction honoring the Sabbath or a festival, usually said over wine

kiddush hashem: (lit. "sanctification of the Name") an act that brings honor to the name of God; martyrdom

kippah (pl. *kippot*; Yiddish: *yarmulke*): skullcap

kohen (pl. *kohanim*): priest; descendant of the ancient Jewish priestly caste

kosher: fit for use according to the requirements of Jewish law

Marrano: a crypto-Jew in Spain or Portugal during or after the Inquisition

mikvah (pl. *mikva'ot*): ritual bath

minyan (pl. *minyanim*): quorum for prayer or other ritual activities

mitzvah (pl. *mitzvot*): (lit. "commandment") a religious obligation; a deed that fulfills a religious obligation

Musar: a movement for moral education in the yeshivot of eastern Europe during the nineteenth and early twentieth centuries; the literature of this movement

niddah: a menstruating woman; menstruation; a tractate of the Talmud dealing with this subject

noi mitzvah: (lit. "beautification of the commandment") the esthetic embellishment of the way a religious obligation is carried out

pe'ah (pl. *pe'ot*): sidelocks

Sages (Hebrew: *Hakhamim, Hazal*): the rabbis of the Talmudic era

seder (pl. *sedarim*): the ceremonial meal of the first night(s) of *Pesah*

sefer Torah (pl. *sifrei Torah*): the handwritten scroll of the Pentateuch used ceremonially in the synagogue

Sephardi (pl. *Sephardim*): a Jew of Mediterranean extraction, especially one whose ancestry can be traced back to Spain or Portugal; of or pertaining to the culture of the Mediterranean Jewish Diaspora

Shabbat (pl. *Shabbatot*; Yiddish: *Shabbos, Shabbosim*): the Sabbath

shehitah: slaughter of animals according to Jewish law

Shmoneh-Esreh: (lit. "eighteen") a silent meditation consisting of eighteen benedictions (plus one added later) that forms a central part of the weekday liturgy

shofar (pl. *shofrot*): ram's horn

shohet (pl. *shohtim*): a ritual slaughterer

siddur (pl. *siddurim*): the Jewish prayer book, especially that containing the liturgy for ordinary days and the Sabbath

sifrei kodesh: sacred books

sukkah (pl. *sukkot*): an open-air hut constructed for use during the festival of *Sukkot*

tahorat hamishpahah: (lit. "family purity") the system by which marital relations are restricted in relation to the menstrual cycle

tallit (pl. *tallitot*; Yiddish: *tallis, talleisim*): prayer cloak

tallit katan: a small, tassled undergarment, worn over the shoulders

talmid hakham (pl. *talmidei hakhamim*): (lit. "disciple of the wise") a learned person

Talmud: the complex, multivolume compilations of legal discourse and lore produced by the rabbis of Babylonia and Jerusalem during the first half-millenium of the common era, especially that of the Babylonian rabbis

talmud Torah: the study of Torah; an elementary school devoted to religious study

tefillin: phylacteries

terumah: tithe

tevilah: ritual immersion

Torah: the Pentateuch; the entire body of Jewish sacred tradition, especially the Bible and the Talmud and their respective commentaries and legal codifications

tref, trefah: (lit. "torn") food unfit for consumption under Jewish law

tsni'ut: (lit. "modesty") a set of norms governing conduct (especially dress) that could be sexually provocative

tzedakah: (lit. "righteousness") charity

tum'ah: ritual impurity

yeshivah (pl. *yeshivot*): an academy of Jewish study, particularly one devoted to talmudic learning

yom tov (pl. *yamim tovim*; Yiddish: *yontev, yontoyvim*): a major holy day, other than the Sabbath

Suggestions for Further Reading

Artscroll's Tanach Series. Brooklyn, NY: Mesorah Publications, 1976–.

Donan, Hayim H. *To Be a Jew*. New York: Basic Books, 1972.

——. *To Pray As a Jew*. New York: Basic Books, 1980.

Ganzfried, Solomon. *Code of Jewish Law: Kitzur Shulhan Arukh*. Brooklyn, NY: Hebrew Publishers, 1961.

The Hertz Bible. New York: Soncino Press, 1958.

Kaplan, Aryeh. *Handbook of Jewish Thought*. Brooklyn, NY: Maznaim Publishing Corp.

——. *Sabbath: Day of Eternity*. New York: NCSY Books, Union of Orthodox Jewish Congregations of America, 1984.

——. *Tefillin*. New York: NCSY Books, Union of Orthodox Jewish Congregations of America, 1986.

——. *Tzitzith: A Thread of Light*. New York: NCSY Books, Union of Orthodox Jewish Congregations of America, 1984.

——. *Waters of Eden: The Mystery of the Mikveh*. New York: NCSY Books, Union of Orthodox Jewish Congregations of America, 1982.

Kitov, Eliyahu. *The Book of Our Heritage*. New York: Feldheim Publishers, 1978.

Lamm, Norman. *A Hedge of Roses: Jewish Insights into Marriage*. New York: Feldheim Publishers, 1977.

Neuwirth, Yehoshua. *Shemirat Shabbat: A Guide to the Practical Observance of Shabbat*. New York: Feldheim Publishers, 1984.

Index